You've Got Mail,
Billie Letts

You've Got Mail, Billie Letts

by
Molly Griffis

EAKIN PRESS ⚜ Austin, Texas

To Mattie—
the best mama-in-law
any girl ever lucked into!

For CIP
information,
please access:
www.loc.gov

FIRST EDITION
Copyright © 2001
By Molly Griffis
Published in the United States of America
By Eakin Press
A Division of Sunbelt Media, Inc.
P.O. Drawer 90159 ⌨ Austin, Texas 78709-0159
email: eakinpub@sig.net
⌨ website: www.eakinpress.com ⌨
ALL RIGHTS RESERVED.

1   2   3   4   5   6   7   8   9

1-57168-313-5 PB

Autographs

When ordinary authors autograph ordinary books, they open to any one of the first few pages, find a nice white spot, and sign their names. But as you have no doubt noticed, *You've Got Mail, Billie Letts* is no ordinary book. Therefore, we felt it fitting that an entire page be set aside for signing by not only the author but also by a couple of the major actors in the stories themselves. Molly insisted that she did not want to show favoritism and therefore requested that the list be done alphabetically, assuring us that it never once occurred to her that Sister's last name was Vineyard.

MOLLY LEVITE GRIFFIS

BILLIE LETTS

GEORGANN LEVITE VINEYARD
(AKA Sister)

Cast of Characters
(quite literally)

Billie—Letts. The reason Molly wrote the Letts Letters. The reason God made Oklahoma. The roller-skating carhop turned author who cannot tell a lie. Or the truth either. At least not very often. Best-selling author of *Where the Heart Is* and *The Honk and Holler, Opening Soon*, and an Oklahoman.

Molly—She had a mama who twirled the truth lightly on the tips of long manicured nails, and a daddy who told the truth and nothing but. Her mama was a flapper and flighty; her daddy was somber and unflappable. Mama wrote checks, and Daddy wrote stories. Molly is a finely tuned combination of both. She is an eccentric lady who owns an eclectic book and blanket shop (Levite of Apache) in Norman, Oklahoma. And she writes letters.

Louis—The only man alive crazy enough to marry Molly not once but twice. Some people never learn.

Dennis—Another glutton for punishment, just like Louis, but he is married to Billie, not Molly. And he only did it once.

Sister is . . . well, she's Sister. Not just to Molly but to those who know Molly because they are jealous and they all want a sister just like her. But she's a Limited Edition of One Only.

Mattie—The dedication to this book explains that Mattie is Molly's mother both in-and-out-of-law. They have the same initials so they can both use the same handkerchief. But they don't.

The offspring who could and did (literally and figuratively):
George and Ginger Griffis
Tracy and Shawn Letts

Introduction

Fellow Letter Lovers,

When Billie and I started corresponding some four years ago, neither of us ever dreamed that our epistles would wing their way onto the pages of a book. Both of us love the written word, so we simply wrote to amuse each other and to form a friendship.

Since neither of us speaks computerese, the current e-mail virus did not infect us. In fact, all of Billie's letters to me were handwritten with no thought of their ever being seen by any eyes other than mine. I was the blatant exhibitionist (my husband's term for my brand of living) who started faxing my letters to friends who, like Billie, laughed at my stories and encouraged me to give them wider exposure.

When *You've Got Mail, Billie Letts* was accepted for publication, my editor asked if I thought Billie would consent to having her letters printed along with mine. To my delight she graciously agreed. Hers is the whipped cream on my cake.

So, look over our shoulders and remember what it felt like to open a real mail box, pull out a real envelope, tear it open, and read a real letter.

Molly Levite Griffis

When we get to know each other better, I want to get a look at the shape of your ears.

January 6, 1996

Dear Billie,

It was great to meet you yesterday, although I will now admit I was tempted to look around for the toadstool you had come out from behind. Am I the only person who thinks you look a lot like an elf? Your red hair and that green dress added to that mystique, I think. When we get to know each other better, I want to get a look at the shape of your ears.

I've had lots of authors come into my little bookshop in my time, but as I told you, they were all self-published and looking for someone to sell their wares. You are the first real live major publishing house person, even if you are an elf look-alike. I am very flattered that you think that Levite of Apache can help put *Where the Heart Is* on the Oklahoma literary "map." I read Novalee's tale of triumph last night and far into the morning. She is my kind of girl!

You said you had been told that my book signings and promotions were a tad bit unorthodox. 'Tis true, 'tis true, but we do draw a crowd. I once had a live buffalo in the shop when we issued a bison book, but she refused to sign a single copy. No matter—all three of the state's major television stations came, and Buffy made all the newspapers, so we sold a ton of books. When a reporter asked my husband how we always managed to draw such crowds, my better half replied, "Blatant exhibitionism."

I am arranging for someone to give birth here in the shop during your signing next month,* but it may need to be an all-day affair since births are often a bit unpredictable.

Are you sure you want my help?

Love,
Molly

[*Novalee Nations, heroine of *Where the Heart Is*, gives birth in a Wal-Mart.]

*. . . keeping the number of computer kills
a secret is just one more
government cover-up.*

January 9, 1996

Dear Billie,

As you are about to discover, I am an inveterate letter writer. Real letters, not those wimpy, peck-'em-out-in-twenty-seconds, one-size-fits-all e-mail things people get so excited about these days. I am a charter member of the Lead Pencil Club and swear that "fingers which touch keys (computer, that is) will never be these." There really is such a club, you know. I sell *Minutes of the Lead Pencil Club* in my little bookstore. Next to your number-one best seller *Where the Heart Is*, it is my most popular title.

Being number one on Levite of Apache's best seller list is nothing to be sneezed at, Ms. Letts. *USA Today* often follows my lead! (Or is that "lead"? I love heteronyms! When I taught 8th grade I always had a contest to see which kid could find the most. Tear, tear. . . wind, wind. . . they filled pages with them, and that led right into a study of context clues!)

I will confess that I *do* own a computer. Ginger, my red-haired daughter, willed it to me when she got a new one. It sits on a desk in the back of my shop, the shame of it obscured from customers by a Pendleton blanket hanging on a rack in front of it. When I have to dash past that evil Cyclopic eye, it crouches like the beast that it is, ready to pounce on anybody who dares to plug it in.

While Ginger assures me that not a single person has ever been injured or killed by an exploding computer, I don't believe her. The way I see it, keeping the number of computer kills a secret is just one more government cover-up. Since our own vice president keeps babbling about the "Super Highway to the Future," do you think the government would let it out that computers kill and maim in great numbers on a daily basis? Bill Gates has enough money to buy off a lot of people.

Anyway, I write real letters every day, often to complete strangers who, I am sure, need me to tell them something. Just as you need me to tell you stories from time to time. When you get famous, we'll call them "The Letts Letters" and publish them to great acclaim. Then, when you become really famous and powerful, you can abolish computers.

Let's hope this all happens before the Millennium meltdown.

Until next time,
Molly

"To my very best friend."

January 11, 1996

Dear Billie,

Did you notice that I spelled your name "Letz" on the first two letters?? I hope not! People always misspell Griffis, thinking it ought to be Griffin or Griffith because they have seen those names before but they have never seen Griffis. It doesn't bother me, but it drives Louis nuts. He is a stickler for detail. My motto is "It will never show on a galloping horse." Louis' reply to that is "You have never been on a horse in your life." Which is true. Your last name does lend itself to some interesting advertising possibilities. We could put signs on buses which read, "Billie Letts You. Some People Won't." I bet that would be remembered.

I got hold of Jamie Raab, the contact you gave me at Warner Books, and she was great! They'll help me with the p.r. stuff for the autograph party you and I discussed when you were here. How about 3:00 to 5:00 on February 3? Since your school visits at Norman High and the Arts and Humanities talks are the 2nd and 3rd of February, you'll already be in

3

town. Saves you the long drive from Durant here just for my event. Although I'll warn you, when I have an event, the people come.

You don't mind signing "To my very best friend" on all of your books, do you? I say that with a smile because I had a lady request that of my wonderful author Harold Keith, who will be ninety-three in April. He was here signing one day, and I had asked the customer if she would like him to personalize it, meaning, of course, did she want "To Mary" or some name. And she said, "Would you put 'to my very best friend'?" To which Mr. Keith replied, "Madam, I've never seen you before in my life." I had a very hard time keeping a straight face.

So, I'll be sure to give you time to form some fast friendships before you sign each book we sell.

Mine will be the very first copy, because I feel we are fast becoming very best friends.

Let me know about the date so I can start planning.

Molly

Have you ever thought of having a signing in a Wal-Mart?

January 13, 1996

Dear Billie,

Glad to get your call this morning.

Plans for your autograph party at my shop are rolling along nicely. What other ones do you have scheduled for this spring? Have you ever thought of having a signing in a Wal-Mart? Personally, Wal-Mart isn't a favorite with me because they were and are so hard on small-town independent stores like my dad's, but I know we could really get some great publicity if you signed there, so I would lower my standards and help! I would think that they would jump at the chance ... you portray Sam Walton as a kind and generous man, so I'm sure they'd approve of his character.

Here's what you do. The next time you are going through some small Oklahoma town, stop and introduce yourself to the manager and suggest a signing. You'll have better luck in a small store rather than in one of those Super Centers, I'm thinking. My best signings have been in little towns because the people don't have anything else to do on Saturdays, and they are flattered that a real live author will take the time to visit their town. Give it a try and let me know when and where, and I'll take care of the publicity for you.

Novalee has been running around in my head ever since I finished your book. You really breathed life into those folks. I especially love Sister Husband. I have a Sister, too, but she's my real live sister whose real live name is Georgann. But I call her Sister, and so do all my friends. And since you are now my "very best friend," you can call her Sister, too. Do you have a sister? If not, I'll share mine with you!

Molly

Rejected by Wal-Mart!

January 15, 1996

Dear Billie,

When I suggested to you that you have an autograph party in a Wal-Mart store, I had no idea what a wonderfully wiggly can of worms I was opening! Rejected by Wal-Mart! How wonderful! I was so excited when you called in such a rage, I didn't get the facts all straight. It doesn't really make sense, especially since Sam Walton was a good character in the book. He even gave Novalee a job!

5

You say you talked to that Wal-Mart manager about having a signing, and he agreed to it. Then, the next day he called you back to say that he couldn't do it, right? If I understood you correctly, he said when he tried to order copies of *Where the Heart Is*, he found that Wal-Mart has chosen not to stock it. That is absolutely marvelous. As I told you, when I tried to sell them the titles I published, I learned that they demand such a hefty discount that I could not afford to deal with them. Because of that deep discount, you would not make nearly as much from their sales as from other bookstores which ask only 40%. So who needs them?

As I told you, when Wal-Mart moved into my folks' little part of Oklahoma, it was the beginning of the end for Levite's in Apache. To his eternal sorrow, my father soon found that he could buy merchandise at Wal-Mart cheaper than he could buy it wholesale. All the little stores were soon devoured.

So I'm not sorry Wal-Mart isn't stocking your book. And I'll bet you that someday, they'll be sorry, too.

To paraphrase Elisa Doolittle, "Just you wait, Sammy Walton. Just you wait!"

M.G.

"Not commercial enough ..."

January 16, 1996

Dear Billie,

I spent the day pondering why Wal-Mart has chosen not to carry your book. The reason they gave, "not commercial enough" seems to me to be a rather cryptic phrase. In fact, it sent me to both my dictionary and my thesaurus.

Here's how *Webster's II New Riverside University Dictionary* defines "commercial" as might apply to *Where the Heart Is*: "1 c. Involved in work designed or planned for the mass market ... [Wal-Mart doesn't think it was written for the

6

masses or they don't consider it a mass market book? Hummm.] 2. Designating products, often unrefined, made and distributed in large quantities for industrial use. [If they carry only 'refined' books, we don't want to deal with them anyway.] 3. Having profit as a primary aim. [Wal-Mart doesn't think they could make enough PROFIT from it? Ah-ha!]"

Now to my thesaurus, looking under "commercial": "Syn. monetary, for profit, pecuniary, materialistic, investment, mundane, prosaic, profit-making, money-making."

Now we know. Wal-Mart does not think they could make enough from selling *Where the Heart Is*. That depends on your meaning of "enough," don't you think? I'd be willing to bet they change their mind someday. And if they do, I certainly won't sell to them!

An inquiring mind,
Molly

She was. And is. My sunshine.

January 24, 1996

Dear Billie,

Just finished my two-mile walk-talk with Sister and as always after that experience, I feel exhilarated. Her happy prattle is my sunshine. I'm sure I've told you that almost every day we walk and talk and listen to each other on tape recorders. We hold the recorder that is playing in our left hand and the one that is recording in our right. That way we can talk, walk, listen, and reply. And the recorders act as our weights!

People we pass think we're strange when and if they realize we are talking into the air rather than into a cellular phone. One day I was striding past a construction site babbling away, and a bricklayer I passed gave me a very puzzled look.

"Oh," I explained, flashing my left-hand recorder, "this is my sister."

He looked at my hand intently and backed away quickly, obviously feeling very sorry for a demented woman who thought a tape recorder was her sister.

Anyway, we rarely miss a day walking because we don't want to miss a story. I have convinced her that the tapes self-destruct in five days if not played (Sister's always been very gullible), so rain or shine we walk and talk. She has a tread-mill but I don't, so I do my walking in the mall if the weather is really, really bad. The other mall walkers avoid me, I might add.

Today Sister was in her prime, recounting our crawdad fishing days. As you have noted, Sister and I have always been close. In spite of the six years between us, when we were lit-tle she always let me tag along. Even crawdad fishing, where I could never keep my mouth shut or quit throwing rocks and horse apples into the creek. That scared off lots of crawdads, but summertime was endless so we just ate animal crackers and waited for the water to settle.

Today she reminded me how I used to snitch Daddy's white cotton handkerchiefs to use to seine for the crawdads. The shelf in the bathroom where the handkerchiefs were kept was nice and low, making them easy prey. A short supply sergeant such as I had to be resourceful. While Sister could be sucked into doing ornery things, I was always the idea guy.

When we finished crawdading, I would try to rinse the handkerchiefs out at the faucet on the east side of the house out of Mama's line of sight. But the soggy mud-stained mess I eventually buried in the middle of the laundry hamper still smelled pretty gamey. Mama, who washed clothes every day of her life even if there were funerals to attend, would haul the dirty clothes out, stuff them in the Bendix, pour in the Duz in the opening on top, and press the start button. Did you all have a Bendix? They were round machines and had an equally round glass window in the round door. I often made a game of sitting on the kitchen floor in front of that all-seeing eye to watch the soap bubbles ride back and forth on wash water waves. I played like it was a Cyclops. We had to make our fun where we could find it in Apache. Probably up there in Tulsa you had whole laundromats filled with Cyclops. You city kids had all the luck.

Anyway, Sister painted me a mental picture of our crawdading days that put all five of my senses on overload. And she reminded me how a day or two after each crawdad adventure, Daddy would complain at the supper table that his handkerchiefs smelled like fish, and he'd wonder aloud what could be the reason.

Mama Lilly, who had her suspicions but kept them to herself, pointed out that the Anadarko water always smelled like fish and that probably some of their water supply got mixed up with our water supply, an explanation that was hardly in the realm of possibility. But Mama's logic often made little sense, so Daddy never pursued it.

Meanwhile, Sister and I would bury our faces in our Fiesta water glasses and try not to make the milk come out of our noses laughing. We always sat at the same spot at the table, and when she left for college it was months before I could look at her empty chair without crying. And when I got a handkerchief, I cried even harder because the handkerchiefs smelled like fish.

When I relived that on my walk today, I told Sister that, as always, she was my sunshine. And to prove it, I sang "You Are My Sunshine" in its entirety on the tape for her.

She was. And is. My sunshine.

And so are you!

Autograph party plans are humming!

Love,
Molly

"How's your day going, Summer Dawn?"

January 26, 1996

Dear Billie,

Yesterday I left you with the happy strains of "You Are My Sunshine" ringing in your ears. Well, here is the sequel to that story.

Last week when it finally stopped raining (we set a record of some kind), Sister ventured to her local K-Mart to wander a few aisles. When she took her purchases to the checkout counter, Summer Dawn (it said so on her name tag right above "Smile If I've Been Helpful") was waiting to take her money.

"What a pretty name," says Sister, who always loves to chat and is in a pretty fine mood. "How's your day going, Summer Dawn?"

To which Summer Dawn replies, "Much better now that the sun is out. There are two things I really hate. The first one is people who say 'Summer's Over!' when they see my name tag, and the second thing on my hate list is rain. I hate rain. I'm a sunshine girl myself. Can't stand all that rain."

Sister, who has just finished listening to me singing on my tape, saw what is known as a "window of opportunity" and whipped out her tape recorder, rewound it, and played my horribly off-key rendition of "You Are My Sunshine" for Summer Dawn. Right there in the checkout line at K-Mart, with the line growing ever longer behind her. Then, while the line lengthened even more, Sister explained to Summer Dawn about our tapes.

Summer Dawn was impressed.

"I wish I had a sister," she said wistfully. "I'm an only." Sister said Summer Dawn paused a minute and then added, "But I call my mother every day, and we talk for twenty minutes."

"Where does your mother live?" Sister asked.

"Right here in town," says Summer Dawn, "but I still call

10

her every day. My old man is always griping at me, sayin',
'Why do you have to call your old lady EVERY DAY?' And I
say to him, 'Because SHE listens.'"

Sister said Summer Dawn kind of stared off into space
and then added, "You know, you really, really need somebody
to ask you every day how your day went and then really listen
when you tell 'em."

Sister allowed as to how that was the truth. It really,
really was.

That's exactly why we do the tapes! We talk and know
that somebody is listening.

Sister and I may vote to adopt Summer Dawn just like
we'll do you, if you want us to.

Nobody should have to be an "only."

You'll get to meet Sister next week!

Love,
Molly

It was better than the story in the Kotex box . . .

February 7, 1996

Hello, again,

Well, I've been so busy being with you that I haven't had
time to write. Wasn't it grand? All the reports I hear on your
school visits were great. And my autograph party was super!
Sorry the weather did not cooperate better, but you know
Oklahoma in February.

After you left, Sister and I voted and you won. You are
now officially our sister, but we'll spell you with a little "s" so
you don't get mixed up with Sister with a big "S." After all,
she is six and one-half years older than we are. She only looks

younger than I because she paints her hair. And I'm not so sure that you don't do that too, right? I am the only natural in the bunch.

Speaking of hair, do you remember the first naughty thing you ever read? In your speeches you talk about reading *God's Little Acre* when you were quite young. Is that the truth, or as you often say, do writers ever tell the truth? Would it be any fun if they did? The first naughty thing I read was in a Mickey Spillane novel. I can't remember the title, but it was the one where the girl was trying to keep him from killing her, so she took off her clothes, piece by piece, and when she stepped out of her panties, it said something like "she was a natural blond . . ." and that totally blew my mind when I realized that he was talking about her pubic hairs, for goodness sake! I read it over and over about twenty times. It was better than the story in the Kotex box my mother read me when I was thirteen. That Kotex booklet had the word "penis" in it, and I didn't know that such things were written down. I've told you before when we talked in person, Sister and I had really, really, really sheltered childhoods.

I think it very sad that children are not sheltered anymore. The times being what they are, they need all the sheltering they can get, but there does not seem to be much shelter left.

Love,
Molly

She would have run away with Leland if she had not been so pure.

February 10, 1996

Billie,

Sister wants you to know about Leland Flinn. She would have run away with Leland if she had not been so pure. She had often told me that if she had followed her gut instinct back in 1947, she would have jumped on the back of Leland Flinn's Harley and taken off for parts unknown. Leland had tattoos and rode the biggest Harley in the state of Oklahoma. Pure as she was (memory is a great censor, it is said) she was pretty certain that other parts of Leland were big, too, but she wasn't quite sure what was done with those parts.

The very fact that he asked her was amazing considering the social standing of our family. He knew that Sister always had to walk on the north side of Main Street so she wouldn't hear the bad language that came out of the South Side Pool Hall, most of it from the lips of Leland and his friends. That's how pure Sister was.

She didn't jump on the back of that Harley, but on her tape to me today she told me to tell you about Leland and his offer. She explained that she wanted you to know that Leland had asked her because she hopes you might put her and Leland in a book someday and have her say "Yes!"

Sister is not nearly as pure as she looks.

Love,
Molly

Nobody likes a showoff.

February 20, 1996

Sister Billie,

I got a new car! A Buick Riviera. We drove all over the state looking for the color I wanted, candy apple red. We found it at Winkler Motor Company in Pauls Valley. I must admit that I have been more than a bit uppity about showing it off to all my friends. I park it right in front of the store and run out and dust it frequently. I did draw the line when Louis suggested an 8 foot by 3 foot banner which read "This is

13

Molly's car. BE IMPRESSED!" I thought about that awhile but finally decided it was a bit tacky. Nobody likes a showoff.

I did, however, get taken down a peg or two last week. The movie company that has optioned one of the books I published sent a scriptwriter here to scope out the territory for film sites. I had been told that she was a 30-year-old Harvard graduate.

"Well," I say to myself as I am awaiting her arrival and feeling just a tad bit intimidated, "so she's a fancy Hollywood type. So she went to Harvard. So she's young and no doubt slender. I bet she doesn't drive a Buick Riviera!"

She arrived at my door having parked her tiny little rental car next to my candy apple red Riviera. She didn't mention my beautiful, fantastic Buick right away, but I decided that was because she was waiting to fall all over herself when she was getting in it to go to dinner.

We exchange formalities and I suggest we go get in my . . . drum roll . . . NEW CAR and drive to the restaurant. I draw myself up to my full 5 foot 4 inches of pride and wait as she circles the back of my vehicle.

"Oh. . . a Winkler," says she, reading the little dealer sticker on the lower left-hand corner of the trunk. "I've never heard of a Winkler. Who makes it?"

"Winkler is an Oklahoma car company," I say with a sigh. "Winklers are very exclusive. This is a limited edition."

"Oh, well," says she with a wan smile. "Are we ready?"

That story should keep you humble when some fancy Hollywood screenwriter is messing with *Where the Heart Is*.

Winkle on!
Molly

Every time she told it, we all held our breath.

March 26, 1996

Dear Billie,

Pour yourself a cup of tea and "set a spell." I imagine you need to prop your feet up, too. Anybody who's going at the clip you are these days needs time for a sinkin' spell.

I read in *The Norman Transcript* that your friend Brad Cushman is going to give a lecture at Norman Public Library April 11. I'm going to go hear him so you might want to warn him that I'll be in the audience and report any bad conduct to you and Dennis.

When Sister and I were giggling our way through the night after we had dinner with you in Tulsa, she was still laughing about my Sally Rand story. You remember you told me that I ought to write it down. I got to thinking and remembered that I had written it down, but I could not for the life of me remember when or why. Then, in the middle of the night, I woke up with one of those light bulbs over my head like you see in cartoons, and I remembered that it was in a letter, of course.

I told you that I am a compulsive letter writer (the last of a dying breed, I might add). That Sally Rand story was in a letter I wrote to Patty Lou Floyd some years ago. I am usually too busy doing other things to keep copies of anything, but in this case I had kept a copy. I am sure Patty Lou will not mind my sharing it with you. Do you know her? She wrote *The Silver DeSoto* which was published by Council Oak. She lives in Tulsa, or at least did when I knew her. You'd love *The Silver DeSoto* as it is a *Where the Heart Is* kind of heart warmer. If you haven't read it, let me know and I will "gift" you with a copy as I sell it in the shop.

Anyway, here's the story you told me to write which I remembered I had already written!

Read On!
Molly

15

Dear Patty Lou,

Sales of *The Silver DeSoto* are flourishing! It is a truly fine book. When I got to the description of rush week at the state university, I laughed so hard my belly hurt. Those were the days, my friend, and you captured them perfectly.

To tell you the truth, I bought your book because your name is Patty Lou. The only other Patty Lou I ever knew was (and still is, I hope) the best storyteller in Apache Grade School in the 1940s. Since you share her name, I figured you had to be good. And sure enough, you are!

She was a redhead, our Patty Lou, and could keep every one of her fellow first graders enthralled for the entire 15 minutes of recess. We'd rather listen to Patty Lou than to skip rope. Or play jacks. Or throw horse apples at the second graders, an activity strictly forbidden and therefore indulged in often.

Patty Lou's best and most often requested story concerned her family's trip to the State Fair of Oklahoma, where they ALL attended a performance of the famed exotic dancer Sally Rand. Now, more than likely it was really Shelly Rand, Sally's not-so-famous cousin, but Patty Lou said it was Sally, and we believed her. We had seen pictures of Sally Rand and her feathered fans in *Life* magazine even though our parents tried to hide that issue. But Patty Lou's folks took her to a live performance! You can easily see why we loved this story best.

Our eyes were wider than Sally's fans, as Patty Lou set the scene.

"We went into this great big tent," she began, making a huge circle with her skinny little arms to show the shape. "It was full of wooden folding chairs just like the ones in the basement of the First Baptist Church." That description caused me to immediately visualize Sally's performance taking place IN the basement of the First Baptist Church, a tantalizing thought, indeed. I kept wondering what the preacher would have to say about it.

"They had church chairs at a strip show?" Billy Clyde wanted to know. Billy was a grade ahead of us, but when the rumor got around that Patty Lou was going to tell all, he crowded in at the back of what was a pretty big circle of kids.

"I didn't say they WERE church chairs, I just said they LOOKED like church chairs," Patty Lou chided. "And it wasn't a strip show. Sally Rand is a lady. Do you want to hear this story or not?"

"Shut up, Billy Clyde," Paul told him. "We don't care about the chairs!" We all got very quiet.

"Well, there was a big red velvet curtain and all of a sudden, right in the middle where it came together, a foot appeared, and on that foot was the most beautiful pink satin slipper in the world. It had a fluffy, puffy ball of real fur on the tip of it . . ."

"There ain't no kind of real fur that is pink," Billy Clyde said disgustedly. "You're making this whole thing up."

"Billy Clyde, I'm gonna give you a knuckle sandwich if you don't keep your trap shut," Paul threatened him.

"Well, then the rest of Sally appeared, but she was all covered up from head to toe with fans, lots and lots of fans, and they were all made of feathers and they were all different colors. She looked just like a peacoct," Patty Lou enthused. Every time she told this, she said "peacoct" but nobody ever giggled or corrected her. We didn't dare.

At this point, Patty Lou would sway back and forth in a kind of bump and grind rhythm to imaginary music, but she never left the center of her stage. "She danced and danced around and around for a long time, dropping her fans as she went along, but she always moved them so fast and there were so many of them, that you never ever could see *nothin'* of what she had on behind those fans." Her voice got lower and lower.

That word "nothin'" stuck in all of our minds.

"Then, she got down to just two fans, the two biggest ones. Both of them were pink, just like her shoes. Her hands were crossed right over her belly button (We were always amazed to hear that Sally Rand HAD a belly button) and she leaned way, way back and pulled those two pink fans apart . . ."

We all held our breath. Every time she told it, we all held our breath.

"And all she had on was three Band Aids!"

Three Band Aids. It boggled our minds. Three Band Aids.

Because of her story, I would bet the farm that to this day not one member of Miss Mabel Eckstein's first grade class puts on a Band Aid without thinking of Patty Lou and her story.

That's power.

Best wishes!
Molly Griffis

March 31, 1996

Dear Molly,

Las Vegas did <u>not</u> hold me in warm embrace! But it is wonderful to be home for a few days.

I so enjoyed my time with you and Sister! You are <u>really</u> <u>special</u> <u>people</u>. (And I'm still laughing and telling friends the "fill 'em up" story.)

Thank you for the lovely dinner—the food was <u>great</u> and the company was <u>splendid</u>. Dennis regrets that he wasn't with us.

I don't know when I'll see you again, but I trust it won't be too long. I'll need a "Molly Griffis fix" soon.

Love to you,
Billie

Thanks for sending the article—It's fantastic!

April 8, 1996

Dear Molly,

I <u>love</u> your Sally Rand story—and in spite of the typewriter "prone to misspell words," it's terrific—well-told, well-written. Get it published! Thanks, too, for the articles, especially the one about Cave-Man Books. (Actually, that's the reason for the <u>quick</u> postcard. I'm several chapters into my new book ... *Cave Girl: Pebbles Chiffon*.) You write <u>great</u> <u>letters</u>! The problem with that is, the people who receive them can <u>never</u> throw them away. Not <u>ever</u>!

My life continues its strange twists. Dennis is leaving Wednesday for Austin. He's going to be playing LBJ in a new Larry L. King play called *The Dead Presidents' Club*. I'm hoping to spend three weeks in May in Austin. I've just sent first five chapters of my new book to my agent. A painful wait!

Love,
Billie

My boots pinch,
but that's show biz.

April 10, 1996

Dear Billie,

Got up at either 4:00 or 5:00 or maybe 6:00 A.M. Because of daylight savings time, I never know for sure.

Walked two miles while talking a mile a minute to Sister on my tape recorder and listening to her at the same speed. She was explaining about God and the universe. She always does that the week after Easter/Passover et al. She read a *National Geographic* article about Buddha and decided to become one of those. She has never been that before. Good luck to her, I say.

Dressed like a cowgirl because I had a program at Eisenhower Elementary School on the Land Run. My boots pinch, but that's show biz. I put on many button covers which don't match and was sorry Ginger was not here to complain; it takes some of the fun out of life when your kids are not around to embarrass.

Stopped at La Bagaette for sesame bagel and double cappuccino so I would have the strength to face 193 fourth and fifth graders who have to sit on the floor for one hour and listen to me.

Did my program. I was great. They asked a million questions and kept me two hours. My boots didn't hurt as much as their rears.

Came to the shop completely forgetting to stop at the P.O. to mail stuff as I was still listening to Sister, who had decided to join some religion that smokes peyote. I told her she had a problem.

Wrote a blurb for Council Oak Books in Tulsa to use in promo material about *Green Snake Ceremony*, Kim Doner's book which won the same big award that your book won. This is it:

"Illustrator Doner's offbeat sense of humor and

shameless plays on words give readers such belly laughs
they will receive their quota of endorphins for the year. If
having the Green Snake Ceremony brings good health and
good luck, think what reading *Green Snake Ceremony* a
bunch of times will do for book lovers young and old."

Called the travel agency to arrange for plane tickets to
Prague May 23 and home June 3 for Ginger and me to visit
son George.

Sold my own two-year-old coat to a Comanche woman
who insisted she couldn't live without that color and pattern.
They don't make that pattern anymore. Hope it doesn't get
cold again.

Love,
Molly

---

*. . . your books will be winging
their way across the country.*

April 12, 1996

Dear Billie,

I was pleased to get to meet your young friend Brad
Cushman yesterday. He is quite talented and has a great sense
of humor. I can see why you and Dennis are so fond of him. I
hope he follows through with his idea to do the note cards
with pictures of the places in your book. I know I could sell a
bunch of them, as could Shelia at the airport. His preliminary
sketches are intriguing.

That reminds me, don't forget that after you speak and
sign in Ada on the 16th, you are to sign and send a dozen
more autographed copies to Shelia Rushing at Will Rogers
World Airport in Oklahoma City. Thanks so much for doing

that for me. I don't mean to make you my distributor, but if Shelia becomes a fan of yours, a lot of your books will be winging their way across the country. She pushes the Oklahoma books like nobody I have ever seen. Be sure to stop in her gift shop and sign every time you are in the airport, OK?

I was so excited to see Dennis in his TV movie last night! Was Piper Laurie as neat as I've always thought she is? Were you a big movie fan as a kid? We went all the time, sometimes as much as five times a week! Daddy was a movie nut, which was kind of funny because that passion didn't really fit with the rest of his character. You'd have thought my zany Mama would be the one who liked to escape that way, but she only went for the air conditioning!

Love,
Molly

April 15, 1996

Dear Molly—

A fine afternoon and evening in Ada—Didn't sell all the books, but met some interesting people. Jennifer, as you promised, is a sweetheart. We both gave you and Levite of Apache great pub. (I told the story of the convict who thought you were a religion—Hope he wasn't in the audience.)

I mailed the books to the airport this morning. (I was there at 5:00 am, but had to wait until 8:30 when the P.O. opened—)

Hope you have fun (I suppose that should be "had fun") in Texas.

Let me know if Sister opts for Buddha or peyote—I'm thinking of making a change myself.

All goes well here—My agent and my editor both enthusiastic about the first five chapters of my new book.

Brad Cushman loved you—as I knew he would. Who doesn't?

Billie

. . . pregnant for
ninety-nine months!

April 22, 1996

Dear Sister Billie,

Attached is a list of people who do not like me. In case you are getting as forgetful as I, you ended your last letter to me with "Brad Cushman loved you . . . Who doesn't?" The names on the attached sheet are those "who doesn't." Be sure to turn it over!

Speaking of forgetful . . . have you heard the one about the lady who flew to Houston, Texas, to attend the Texas State Library convention last week only to find to her amazement that the Texas Library Convention was THIS week not LAST week?

It was and is I. Talk about embarrassing! Oh, well. Just remember to never ask me if I enjoyed the Texas Library Convention. Luckily, I have tons of relatives in Houston, so I pretended that I was making a surprise visit, but I don't think I fooled anybody.

At one time I had twenty-one Texan first cousins, all from my mother's side of the family. My dad's side were not very prolific, I'm afraid. But Grandma and Grandpa West had eleven, and those eleven took the biblical admonition, "Be fruitful and multiply" seriously. We cousins talk a lot about our poor old grandma when we are together. It is hard to even comprehend being pregnant for ninety-nine months, but she was. Imagine all of those heavy, heavy days with no air conditioning, no washing machine, no refrigerator. How did they do it, those poor pregnant-every-two-years ancestors of ours?

I got a wonderful thank you note from Elizabeth F. Hailey thanking me for the autographed copy of your book. She inscribed it "To my favorite Pendleton blanket-selling book publisher" because I had said in my letter, "You may not remember me but I am the Pendleton blanket-selling book publisher from NORMAN; I say to distinguish myself from other Pendleton blanket-selling book publishers you might have met that were from some place else." I reread her *A Woman of Independent Means* in honor of having met her in person. Her protagonist was certainly nothing like our poor grandmas, was she?

Kaye never questioned why I was in the car trunk.

April 26, 1996

Dear Billie,

It is raining today, the neat kind of rain . . . soaking, slow and pattery. So when my friend Kaye called at 7:30 A.M. to say she needed to swing by my house on the way to the city to get me to witness some document she needed to sign, I decided to wait for her in the trunk of my Winkler. You do remember that my "Winkler" is a Buick Riviera; I just call it a Winkler. [See page 13.]

I probably shouldn't tell you this, but I like to read in the trunk of the car. Not when it's moving, of course, just when it's parked in the garage. No, I don't close the lid. . . the light goes out when you do that. Anyway, as I climb in, I realize that this is my first read in the Winkler trunk, which is much, much smaller than the trunk of that giant, old-people Oldsmobile or the giant green Pontiac which preceded the Olds. I have to lower myself sideways instead of just jumping in as I used to do. This is definitely a challenge.

Once I am in and seated, it's not so bad, but I am thinking to myself that getting out is going to be a little bit tricky. I had brought the garage door opener with me because I thought it would be fun to surprise Kaye, who does not know about my trunk fetish, by opening the garage door when I heard her car drive up in my driveway. I settled down with the morning newspaper.

23

Now, while I was doing all of this, I had forgotten that the guy who delivers our bottled water was due today. We just changed companies, so the schedule is new, and this would be his first time to deliver. I had told the woman who set up the account to have the delivery man come in through the gate in the fence at the side of the house because we keep the empty bottles on the top of the file cabinet in the garage. I had not talked to him in person so had no idea if he were young, old, tall, slim, or most of all understanding of an older woman's idiosyncrasies.

Unaware of impending doom, I am reading away when he parks his truck in the street, so I don't hear the engine. I am first aware of him when I hear the gate being opened, and I freeze trying to decide what to do in order not to scare him to death because the garage is dark from his end, and it might not occur to him that I would be reading in the trunk of my car. So in one of many bad choices I made today, I crawl into the back of the trunk and get in the fetal position, all the while thinking that I simply must get back on my medication if I managed to get out of this alive.

I hear him come in, take down the two empty water bottles, plop the two full ones on the top of the cabinet, and I am about to sigh a big sigh of relief when there is a long pause in sound . . . a long silence. In my mind's eye I see him notice that the trunk of the car is up. And because he was no doubt a Boy Scout in his younger days, he quickly walks to the back of the car, slams the trunk lid down, and exits knowing that he has done his good deed for the day.

Lucky for me it was not long until Kaye arrived, started looking for me, heard me yelling from the car trunk, popped the button in the door which releases the trunk lid and got me out.

Kaye never questioned why I was in the car trunk. She's that kind of friend.

Molly

They stood around waiting for Jane Russell to appear.

May 5, 1996

Dear Billie,

What fun to see you yesterday, even if the circumstances were wild! I was just glad that I was able to make it to Oklahoma City in time to be set up when your speech was over. I broke the speed limit, I will admit, but I was all prepared to tell the cop, "Officer, we have a real book emergency here." I'm sure he would have then escorted me right to you immediately. It would have been pretty bad to not have the speaker's books available for signature after such an important luncheon!

That's not the first time one of the big chains dropped the ball when they were supposed to furnish books at a convention. So many of them are managed by kids who have no vested interest. As you can imagine, I am not usually inclined to bail them out, but when you are involved, that's different. I was just glad that I had plenty of your books in stock.

My only regret is that I didn't have a camera there to take your picture when you saw the poster that Kim and I threw together when you called. It was sheer serendipity that she was here in my shop signing AND that she would have a copy of *People* magazine, which contained that wonderful old photo from the movie *The Outlaw* in living color. Of course it was Kim's idea to cut off Jane Russell's name, insert yours and put it on the poster! But remember, you started it. I have told the story a million times about you sending Warner that sexy photo of Jane Russell reclining in the hay when they requested a cover shot for *Where the Heart Is*. Wish they had used it!

What you missed was two wonderful old codgers who wandered by while I was waiting for you to finish speaking and come sign. They saw the Jane Russell poster and the caption "Now Signing" but did not notice the "Billie Letts" beneath the photo. So they stood around waiting for Jane to appear. I must tell you that they were sorely disappointed when you arrived.

I explained to them that *People* magazine had gotten your photo mixed up with Jane's and that next month they would have a retraction, but that didn't seem to help much.

You well know that I never lie, so start watching *People* for your picture!

Love,
Molly

"I'm $5 ahead!"

May 7, 1996

Sister B.,

I am listening to Sister on my little mini cassette tape recorder this morning and laughing so hard that tears are running down my chubby little cheeks. You know that she and I tape to each other every morning when we walk. We've been doing it for years. In fact, we are such "advanced" tapers, that each of us has two recorders, one to talk into and one to listen to. People passing by think we are either very busy executives or crazy, but we don't care.

Today's happy tears came because sister is telling me about her renter. When Mama died eleven years ago, she left her very nice home and some very tacky rent houses. When Dad was living he kept the rent houses in good shape because he could repair anything, and he checked on them often. But after he passed away, Mom left them to their own devices, and you know what that means.

Sister, who has always been an admirer of Leona Helmsley, decided that she would become a slum landlady and let me have Mama's house, which I promptly sold. I gave Sister half the money, and she said if she ever sold her slums, she'd give me half. Meanwhile, I told her to keep all the rent for the trouble I was sure she was going to have collecting it.

The three places rent for $35 each.

They have no pools, no Jacuzzis. In fact, one has no running water. But the renters have all lived there for years and are happy with their lot.

Billy Bob in particular is happy because he has not paid his rent in eleven years. This is why I am laughing.

Every month Sister writes him nasty letters. Well, not really nasty, but stern.

"Billy Bob," she writes, "if you will send me $70 a month from now on, I will drop $500 from the $4,620 you have owed me for the last eleven years."

She writes him a different deal every month: "Send $50 and I'll forgive $760 . . . Send me $25 and I'll drop $273 . . ." And so on.

Now, once in a while, quite randomly, Billy Bob will drop a check in the mail for random amounts, so she knows he has a checking account. She figures he does this to let her know that he's alive so she won't rent his place to somebody else.

She has, from year to year, tried to confront him in person, but Apache is such a small town that he somehow always knows she's coming, and he's never home. Rumor has it that he spends the rent money paying somebody to watch the road between Lawton and Apache and beep him on his beeper (of course Billy Bob has a beeper!) when they see Sister's car approaching, but I'm not sure that is true. It does make a good story.

On today's tape she reported that she had gotten a Billy Bob check for FIFTY dollars, so she sent him a Hallmark thank-you bouquet which cost her $45. "I'm $5 ahead!" says she.

Love,
Molly

Do you think
they went on eating?

Dear Billie,

The new *Oklahoma Today* magazine has a story by Richard Bedard, the kid you met in my shop last week, which I think you'll enjoy. Everybody who comes in here to buy his book has a tornado story.

"In our town there was a deaf family," a guy said yesterday, "a whole family of them, mother, father, and two kids. All were totally deaf. When that twister hit at 7:04 on February 7, 1961," he recalled with pinpoint accuracy, "they wuz sittin' at the supper table. All a sudden the lights went out and the whole roof wuz taken right off. It was pitch black, and they didn't have no idea what had happened. So they just set there at the table and waited. Took the Civil Defense three hours to find them."

Can you imagine what went through their minds while they sat there? It had been a sunny day. They had not heard the tornado sirens. Do you think they went on eating? What went through their minds, I wonder. The guy telling the story was nine years old in 1961. The town was in your neighborhood, Konawa. You may want to put that in your book. Is there a tornado in it?

I love storytellers! Hadn't thought of the Civil Defense in years. We had them in Apache. Did you have them around Tulsa? When is your new book set—time, I mean?

Ginger and I leave for Prague, the Czech Republic, on May 23 and won't be back until June 3. Do you think you can stand to go that long without a letter from me? Do I need to write up a bunch of letters and have Louis mail them every day or so? You can always trust a man with a crue cut to follow orders. (I either have to learn how to spell that word or he's going to have to let his hair grow out!)

Well, as the operator used to say, "Your three minutes are

up!" My children do not believe it when I tell them that used to happen. It takes them three minutes to say, "Yeah, is that you?"

Love,
Molly

"Rules is rules, Bub!"

May 14, 1996

Billie L.,

Here's a TRUE Wal-Mart story, unlike some Wal-Mart stories I have heard or read.

Judy was my little sister in a college sorority long ago. She was my maid of honor—she married the guy I had brought from Norman to Apache to do my hair for the nuptials. Lest you think I was a pretty fancy bride to have my own hairdresser, he was a kid who had not graduated from high school and was painfully aware of his lack of literary background as he twisted hair in a university town. He did my hair for free and I talked to him in Shakespeare. Not during the ceremony, of course.

Anyway, that's another story for another letter.

Judy married the hairdresser, had two kids, divorced him; married an Indian, divorced him; and finally married a wonderful Jew whose parents had died in concentration camps. Ed, the Jewish guy, had been put on a train to London by his parents before they were shipped away. They had this version of orphan trains back then where they sent the little Jewish kids to England where rich people who wanted a child or wanted to look good went to the station, pointed at a child, and said, "We'll take that one!" That's how Ed got his new family. But that's another story, too.

During the years between divorces, Judy got an R.N. in

29

nursing, a master's in psychology, and finally became a doctor of osteopathy.

She is an interesting person.

She now has a malignant brain tumor and last November was given six months to live.

I have been storming the gates of heaven with pleas for her recovery ever since. She is undergoing every treatment in the world; if anybody can beat the odds, it is she.

Although she has several wigs, she says they are horribly uncomfortable and hot, so most of the time she covers her poor, bald head with a baseball cap and does what has to be done. Like shop at Wal-Mart for groceries.

My sweet little doctor sister was dressed in old blue jeans, a dirty t-shirt, and her baseball cap. No hair.

She overextended herself and realized that she was about to collapse. She had her cart in line and was the next to be rung up when she heard the checker say, not at all kindly, "You got more than ten items, Bub. Git in the other line!"

Dr. Judith Atlee Mitchell Keel Kaswan, who was about to faint, said, "Oh, please, I don't believe I can make it to the other line. Please check me out."

"Rules is rules, Bub! Move it!" says Mother Teresa of the cash register.

"I'm REALLY having a bad day," pleads Judy, clutching the counter. "I really, really am."

"You a truck driver?" the checker wanted to know, looking Judy over carefully from old ball cap down to shoes. "My second old man was a trucker and that's a hell of a life. You remind me of him."

A TRUCK DRIVER?

Judy said she loved that question so much, that it was such a wonderful, wonderful observation on the part of the checker, that she started laughing so hard she got to feeling better immediately.

And the checker decided to check her out even though she had eleven items.

God bless Wal-Mart.

Molly G.

Burning a vehicle
without a permit . . .

June 15, 1996

Dear Billie,

I told the wild story of your pickup burning up to every-body who came in the shop today. Most of them claim to know you because they have read your book. I think it's wonderful that they say, "Oh, yes, Billie Letts. I know her! She wrote that book about the girl having the baby in the Wal-Mart store." They read you. They know you. Do you find it scary that they all think that you are Sister Husband?

Speaking of scary, after we hung up, and I stopped laugh-ing about the dear old sisters across the street to whom you went for help, I got to thinking that the whole event really was pretty scary. Obviously, fire and gasoline can be big trouble. How long did it take the fire department to get there?

I sure hope that when the photographer from *The Durant Daily Democrat* got there to take pictures you had the good sense to grab a couple of copies of *Where the Heart Is* and hold them up when they were shooting. You've got to learn to grab all the free publicity you can get, Billie, if you expect your book to make the best-seller list.

Did they give you a ticket for something? Burning a vehi-cle without a permit, maybe? That would be good, too, because maybe they'd say, "Billie Letts, local author . . ." in the police report.

If they did haul you off to jail, I sure hope they are for-warding your mail.

Molly

Sister's mother-in-law lives.

July 1, 1996

Dear Billie,

Sister had the mother of all mothers-in-law. God rest her soul, she is no longer on this plane, but wherever she is, I'll guarantee you that she makes them uncomfortable. The descriptive word "straight laced" was coined just for her. Lips that touched wine never touched hers, and on and on and on.

But she did like to talk, and picking up new and what she considered "hip" terms or phrases was her specialty, although quite often the terms or phrases were neither new nor hip, nor used correctly.

It was a hot summer day. Sister was looking out the window of her little apartment at a tiny, tiny cloud that was winding its way across a broad expanse of blue Oklahoma sky. "I think it might rain," she says wistfully.

"Oh," replies her visiting mother-in-law, "you're just having a wet dream." And she nods sagely.

For years, Sister and I tell this story and laugh about the poor old lady's naive, wonderfully funny comment.

Quantum leap to last week.

I have made friends with a young man named Rustin who works at Kinko's and who weekly tells me his life story. On Monday he has reported that he has met the girl of his dreams on the Internet. They have talked all night long on the phone after having met on the net. She lives right here in town. He asked her to meet him for breakfast, she did, and they clicked. And on and on.

So, yesterday, I breeze into Kinko's and when I see Rustin, I, who have read all about computers and inner and outer net and have picked up words like "floppy disk . . . cyber space . . . virtual reality . . ." say to Rustin with a wink, "Well, how's your cybersex going?"

He looks so startled and embarrassed and amazed that I

know something has gone wrong, but I don't know what. So I say, "You know . . . that girl you met Sunday night . . . cybersex?"

He mutters something about something and exits to the back, so I copy my stuff, pay another guy, and leave.

I get home and snuggle into my chair to read more of my new book, *Minutes of the Lead Pencil Club*, which has wonderful anti-computer essays by favorites like Russell Baker, Henry David Thoreau, who wrote *Walden Pond* in pencil, and others. Then, I come to a section on definitions of computer terms.

"Cybersex . . ." I read aloud to myself, "masturbating while talking to someone on the net who is doing the same."

Sister's mother-in-law lives. And Rustin knows her.

Love,
Molly

"I've seen it all."

July 3, 1996

Hello out there,

It is a strange world indeed. I often wonder if I am the only person this kind of stuff happens to.

I edit a newsletter for the Cranial Society of Doctors of Osteopathy (don't ask). Monday I had to fax a corrected article to the national president, causing me to make a stop at Kinko's where old cybersex Rustin works.

When I go in, neither Rustin nor I act as if there has been any sexual reference or perversion between us. He is making out my ticket when an older, gray-haired gentleman comes up and says in a rather strained and frantic voice, "I left something in the machine yesterday! Did you find it?"

Something. Machine. That's Rustin's and my only clues.

Rustin keeps a very straight face, does not ask WHAT it was that was left, and pulls a large cardboard box from beneath the counter. "This is the refuse for the past week," he says rather parenthetically, and goes on writing out my ticket.

The man rummages through for quite some time, then finally, reverently, withdraws a piece of paper, sighs a big sigh of relief, and leaves.

I, who have been breaking my neck trying to see what is on this paper, wondering if he Xeroxes the Bible like SOME people I know,* almost fall over the counter, but I can see nothing.

"That great big box is just from one week?" says I.

"You wouldn't believe what people leave in our machines," replied Rustin. "Passports, driver's licenses, Social Security cards, birth certificates, divorce decrees, women's lacy underwear . . ."

"Underwear? People Xerox lacy underwear?" I say to Randy Rustin, thinking perhaps he is paying me back for the cybersex shock of last week.

"Underwear," says he. "I've seen it all."

And I believe him.

Do you think these things happen because I edit that newsletter?

Love,
Molly

[*Sister Husband, a character in *Where the Heart Is*, hands out Xeroxed chapters from the Bible.]

"I thought you didn't eat meat."

July 14, 1996

Dear Billie,

For over ten years, I have not eaten meat in front of Louis nor have I eaten anything sweet in anything but total darkness. I have this theory that these two actions keep me from gaining weight.

The fact that I have gained twenty-three and a half pounds in that same time frame has not changed my theory, only my dress size.

Last Thursday I was staring at the menu of the subshop next door to my store. I eat there once a week. Crystal, the slender, long-legged, shorts-with-cowboy boots wearer, who both owns and waitresses the Penny Hill, prides herself in her good memory as well as her good figure.

If you are a repeater, she grabs for the white or wheat before the door slaps shut behind you. Then she stands there with her slender legs, her cowboy boots, and your loaf waiting to hear your choice. In my case, she waits to hear me say "Turkey" or "Tuna" so she can say, "Your usual way, right?" and smile that damned I-am-not-only-slender-but-I-know everything Ipana smile.

This particular Thursday, Crystal and I were the only two people in the shop, which is usually packed. There were no witnesses, and a person can take just so much slenderness.

"I'll have a B.L.T. on white please. A large one. To go," says I.

"I can't believe it," says Crystal. "I can't believe it."

I don't comment. She makes, I pay, I leave.

I lock the front door to my shop, go to the back behind the curtain, and eat every single crumb.

Since Louis is not only my accountant but also my janitor, I bury the sandwich wrap at the bottom of a box, cover it with plastic popcorn, spray it with bathroom deodorant, and get back to shopkeeping. I feel good.

Yesterday, I had my ninth anniversary celebration of the founding of my company with a gala attended by hundreds perhaps thousands of people including Louis.

I was too busy to eat, or to notice that when noon came, he went next door to grab a sandwich and perhaps Crystal.

He waited until we got home to say, "By the way, Crystal says you had a B.L.T. on white bread. I thought you didn't eat meat."

It goes to show that the slender are not to be trusted. Especially those who wear cowboy boots with shorts.

Love,
Molly

Microwave Squirrel Tail?

July 22, 1996

Dear Billie,

Last Friday at 3:07, this woman walked into my office, plopped her briefcase down on the chair next to my desk, flipped it open, and without as much as a "howdy do" asked, "Is there enough in here for a book?"

More amused than amazed (I've been publishing books for nine years and have had visits from more would-be authors than either Mr. Random or Mr. House), I peered into the case which was stuffed with every size, color, and type of material—typed on white paper, handwritten on lined tablet sheets, xeroxed photos—in a great hodgepodge heap.

"What kind of book?" I say, mentally appraising her tasteful, tailored black suit, her high heels, and her nylon stockinged feet. No straightjacket was apparent.

"It's a cookbook," says she. "A Native American cookbook. I am Chickasaw on my father's side. Got the papers and everything. I have here recipes that have been handed down from generation to generation. Some of them were originally written on buffalo hides, I think," she adds rather parenthetically and she takes a deep breath.

Intrigued by her manner as much as her material, I pick up the paper on top and read aloud. "Microwave Squirrel Tail."

I swear on the nearest Bible, that is what it said: "Microwave Squirrel Tail."

Staving myself from inquiring, "What if my tepee does not have an outlet which will take one of those three-pronged cords," I say, "Hummmm. Microwave Squirrel Tail?" with a bit of a question mark at the end.

"Well, yeah, I have adapted them for modern living." She scratches her nose. "Is there enough here for a book?" she asks again.

"That depends on quite a few things," I say, picking up the next sheet. It is bright pink and on it is printed:

BUY NOW AND AVOID THE RUSH!
COOKBOOK FOR ALL OCCASIONS!
ONLY $12.95
HAVE TO SEE TO BELIEVE!
LIMITED EDITION!

I stop reading and look up at her again. "Oh, I seem to have misunderstood. I thought you were wanting ME to publish this. But I see now that it is a book that has already been published and you are wanting help in marketing it, right?"

"Oh, no. I want you to publish it, sell it, and give me all the money," says she.

I check again for the straightjacket; maybe she had hidden it under the suit coat.

"But where did these fliers come from?"

"Oh, Kinko's was having their half price sale, so I got them real cheap, but I had to do it last week as the sale was about to be over."

"But . . . but . . . how did you determine this price of $12.95 when the printing cost had not been determined? And you have no title, and furthermore . . ."

"Oh, you could sell them for more if you wanted to. You could just mark out that price and put in another one. I only had 5,000 done for starters. They were really cheap. I was thinking about *Tantalizing Tepee Temptations to Tickle the Taste Buds* for the title. What do you think?"

"Well, I . . ."

"If you don't think there is enough here for a book, we could add some of my poetry for fillers," she continues. (I swear I am not making this up. I know that's what that crazy humor columnist says about his newspaper clips, but I'm always sure he IS making it up. Some of my stories I've made up. This one is true.) "We could have a poem on every other page."

"But . . ."

"And if we don't have enough of mine to fill it up, we could use some of Kahlil Gibran's stuff. I really like Kahlil Gibran," and she looks a little dreamy-eyed in thinking of *The Prophet*.

"But you can't use someone else's work without his permission," I feel compelled to say.

"Oh, he's dead," she explains. "He won't care."

Now, I keep a stack of boxes near my desk, a rather large stack, for just such occasions, because it is clear this conversation could go on forever.

"You see those boxes?" I say with great efficiency. "I have to get those to the UPS office by . . ." and I say whatever time is five minutes from the current one . . . "or I'm in really big trouble. Big order. Right from the top. Big order. Got to be out today." And I start gathering up my purse, my checkbook, and other official looking stuff.

"You're making a big mistake turning this down," says she. "My mother says it will probably be a New York Times Bestseller for the publisher smart enough to snap it up."

"Nevertheless," and I head for the door loaded down.

"Mother thinks I might sell more if I called it *The Best of Martha Stewart*, but I don't know about that. I don't think Martha Stewart is Indian at all."

I ease her out the door and suggest she go next door and see if Crystal of the subshop will share her secret recipe for white buns. Crystal, as you may recall, is a big talker.

> They deserve each other.
> Molly

What a deal!

July 25, 1996

Dear Lettses,

I have always wondered about making a surname plural when it ends in an "s" already. Names like Griffis . . . and Letts. Just try saying "Griffises" or Lettses," much less spelling them.

It's not easy.

But neither is making ends meet in this day and time.

My poor Sister is always trying to think of new ways to make a buck now that she and her husband are retired and their income has been cut in half. Her husband has a rather deadly combination: a love of horse races and incredibly bad luck. So they often find themselves lacking in the money department.

That's why, when she read in the newspaper about a lady in one of the New England states who was suing the Catholic church for $4 million, she realized that this was not a Friday. You may or may not remember that Sister belongs to a religion-of-the-week club; on Fridays she is Catholic because it's easy to remember since that used to be fish-in-the-cafeteria day before the Pope waffled. So, not having to say "that's against my religion," she had a wonderful idea.

The New England lady had stated that she was at a Bingo game in the school gym of a local Catholic school, minding her own business, when a scoreboard located right above her head fell and knocked her silly. So silly, in fact, that when she came to and attempted to go on with her life, she found that she now had spontaneous random orgasms, sometimes as many as ten a day.

What a deal! So, of course, she decided to sue the church.

Well, reading about that lawsuit gave Sister the money-making idea of all time.

She would buy a scoreboard, set it up above a chair, and drop it onto the heads of each and every lady willing to plop down fifty bucks for a hit.

What do you think? Is $50 too little? Too much? Just right?

Billie, what would you pay?

Love,
Molly

"I'm so excited my nipples itch!"

July 27, 1996

Dear Billie,

Well, I am getting pretty excited about my trip next week to the writers' convention in Los Angeles (L.A. to those of us "in the loop" or whatever they call it when you are "with it" or "on it" or some such thing). Since this is the 25th Anniversary of the Society of Children's Book Writers and Illustrators, all the really big names will be there ... Judy Blume, E. L. Klonisburg, Eve Bunting ... everybody I have ever read and loved. I'm so excited that my nipples itch.

I wish I could take credit for that line "so excited that my nipples itch." Doesn't it conjure up a great image? It was said to me by a wonderfully funny real-estate saleswoman named Velma Barnes one hot summer day years ago. Velma was known as "that Purple Person" here in Norman because of her love for that particular color. All of her advertising signs were done in purple, she wore nothing but purple clothes, she even drove a purple Cadillac. She was a unique lady.

One day in the summer of 1964 I went into her office to get her to help us find an apartment. Louis had just gotten out of the army, and we were moving back to Norman where I had a job as a graduate assistant in English at the university. My salary was $250 a month, so we needed a very small, very economical place to light until Louis found suitable employment. He had a master's in business and great expectations but no job yet.

Anyway, when I went in, Velma, whom I had never laid eyes on before, but knew by her colorful reputation, greeted me with: "Oh God! I'm so hot my nipples itch!"

I thought it a wonderful line and stole it for my own. Someday it will be the opening sentence of my great American novel, which I plan to start right after I get home from the writers' convention in L.A.

Somehow, I imagine there are lots of itchy nipples in L.A. I'll soon know for sure!

Love,
Molly

I've GOT to remember
to go to the bathroom . . .

July 29, 1996

Billie the Kid,

After I hung up from talking to you, I realized that "There's Lots of Itchy Nipples in L.A." is the perfect title for a country and western song. The tune even started playing in my head. Can't you hear it?

> "There's a lot of itchy nipples in L.A.
> Lots of lonely gals who scratch 'em every day
> While they're cruisin' in a car
> Or sittin' in a bar
> Yes, there's lots of itchy nipples in L.A."

(I've GOT to remember to go to the bathroom before I start composing because I always wet my pants when I laugh.) Oh no! Here comes another one:

> "I always wet my panties when I laugh
> Yes, I always wet my panties when I laugh
> While I'm ridin' in the car
> Or sitting in a bar
> I always wet my panties when I laugh."

See, if you change "cruisin'" to "ridin'" it gives it a whole new flavor.

I'm a sick person, do you know that? And it's all your fault. Why do you inspire me this way? Are you a muse or something?

Molly

P.S. This is too naughty for Dennis' eyes so read it out loud to him. I bet Shawn could write the music.

"Put this is in a box and mail it . . ."

Dear Letts Letter Lovers (a wonderful double entendre!)

I once rented an 8 foot by 8 foot room in the back of Mercury Post and Parcel. I had moved my "publishing house" from my kitchen table to this one little room because Louis said the tax people would be a bit suspicious of my wanting a $12,386.92 deduction for paper clips and pencils if I didn't have a real address different from our home.

My room had no view. No window, in fact.

So I took the trash out a lot, checked to see if the hired help had filled the rented mail boxes, and in general made trips to the front so I could be sure the world was still out there. In so doing, I watched a wonderful parade of folks who brought things in to be mailed. Since Mercury was not a REAL post office where you have to bring things ready to be bent, stapled, and mutilated by the "through snow, sleet, and rain" folks, customers expected more in the way of service. These customers could buy boxes, packing material, and even get the kids behind the counter to wrap for them.

One guy was getting a divorce so he just "swept" everything in his house—repeat EVERYTHING IN HIS HOUSE—into big boxes: dishes, lamps, books, iron, vases, clothes, the works. He filled many, many boxes and brought them down to UPS them to his ex. Well, UPS automatically insures every box for $100, so they wouldn't take them because each box rattled something awful what with all that broken glass which the guy admitted to having smashed in the packing process. He was furious when the kid behind the counter would not accept those boxes.

Students from OU routinely came in after finals with arms loaded with their clothes, STILL ON THE HANGERS, threw them down on the counter along with their DIRTY sheets, pillowcases, and socks, and said, "Send these to my folks COD." as they filled out the necessary forms.

42

My favorite was a man who came in once a month and paid $68.50 to send three six-packs of Diet Dr Pepper to his sister in Alaska. He packed them in a plastic bucket that pickles had come in. She couldn't get Diet in Alaska, he explained, and he loved her a whole lot and didn't want her to get fat.

One elegantly dressed lady in a fur swept in just as I was about to go home for the night. She took off a very beautiful bracelet, placed it on the counter and said, "Put this in a box and mail it to this address . . ." She produced a piece of paper with the information on it . . . "and insure it for $15,000. Here's the appraisal." Then she proceeded to whip off the fur, plop it down on the counter and say, "And mail this to this address . . ." she retrieved another piece of paper from the pocket of the fur . . . "insure it for $50,000. Here's that appraisal." She waited while I stared and the kids made out the proper forms, told her an enormous amount, I forget just what, and she paid in cash. She turned without a word of explanation and left.

As soon as the door snapped shut behind her we pulled the curtain and took turns trying on the coat, which was full length.

Aren't people wonderful?

Molly

This is a goat story.

August 4, 1996

Dear Billie,

This is a goat story. A true goat story. But since your name is Billie, I'm afraid you're going to think that I have made this up especially for you. I have not. It is true.

When my kids were little, I was in charge of the animals for Vacation Bible School at the church we were attending at the time. Since my father was Jewish and my mother Baptist, I have always thought that God speaks all languages. The year we added an addition to our house, our builder was also a Church of God preacher whom we came to admire greatly, so we attended his church. His name (again you are going to have to take a great leap of faith and believe me) was Brother Pharaoh. It was. It really was. Now I will admit that "Brother" was not his given name, but that was what he was called.

Anyway, Brother Pharaoh's church was very fundamental. They wanted to have real animals, the kind which would have been around in the time of Jesus because this particular church was a Christian one, of course.

One of my kids' school teachers owned a goat, and I volunteered to borrow it for Bible school. She was named Nanny by someone totally lacking in imagination. I put Nanny in the van, drove her to the church, and watched while hordes of kids played with her, talked to her, and . . . here comes trouble . . . fed her the remains of their lunches. Goats can digest anything, right? You've heard that all your life, right? Don't believe everything you hear.

Well, Bible school was over for the day, everybody went home, and as I was leaving, a giant thunderstorm began to roll in. Nanny's owner had told me that she was really afraid of thunder. (Nanny, that is, not the teacher.) Nanny started bucking like a bronco, broke the rope, and headed down the street.

Remembering the Bible quote "Do unto others . . . " I made the quick decision that I would not want "others" to allow their goat to run through my flower beds, so I started to chase Nanny, wondering why I had left our previous church which had had a piano and no goat.

In an amazing coincidence, two animal control officers were having lunch at a nearby Arby's, saw Nanny sprinting down the street, and lassoed her. Because serendipity always dances with me, somebody driving by had a kid in Sunday school who recognized Nanny and told the animal control people where she belonged. We all arrived back at the church at the same time.

I signed the necessary papers to reclaim the goat. Nanny had been such a sport that I hated to think of her spending a whole night tied up to a tree outside in a driving rainstorm.

The teacher had told me that Nanny was as house-broken as much as such creatures can be, so I thought we were surely safe until morning. I took her into the kids' Sunday school room, gave her a hug, and left for the night.

Did you know that there is a special word for diarrhea when it is experienced by a goat? Scours. That's what goat diarrhea is called. And that's what Nanny had as a result of all that church food and her K5 run. I really wish I were making this up.

So does the janitor of that church.

It's the only one we were asked to leave.

Love,
Molly

To tell the honest truth (for the first time this year) . . .

August 5, 1996

Sister,

This is really a P.S. rather than a real letter and needs to be read in conjunction with the goat letter, so I hope you just finished it.

Louis has not. Not read the goat letter, that is. To tell the honest truth (for the first time this year), the goat story did not happen to me. It really did happen (with variations), but it happened to my niece Vicky. When she told me, I was laughing so hard thinking of the fun I could have with it because I really did attend Brother Pharaoh's church, he was our builder, and so on, that I forgot the word for goat diarrhea.

I called Vicky to find out the word and got her answering machine. I told the machine what I needed to know and asked Vicky to call me back. Which she did at about ten that night.

Louis had been asleep for some time, and I was reading in

bed next to him when the phone rang. I ran into the den to answer it so he would not be further disturbed. I grabbed a pencil, wrote down "scours," and headed back to bed.

"Who was that?" mutters Louis, who has, you must remember, no knowledge of the goat letter.

"Vicky," says I.

"What did she want?" asks he.

"She wanted to tell me that goat diarrhea is called scours," says I.

There was a rather long period of silence.

"Oh," says Louis, "I see." And he turns over and goes back to sleep.

Do you think being married to me 36 years has dulled his senses?

Molly

"What kind of prizes?"

August 9, 1996

Dear Billie,

Here I am in L.A. scratchin' my nipples and spending money, two of my favorite occupations. There were no postcards in the drawer at this fancy hotel, which is good since these are "The Letts Letters," not "The Letts Postcards." I could never confine my stories to a postcard.

The limo (that's what the famous such as we call them) is taking us to Rodeo Drive, which I have discovered is not a place where cowboys rope steers, but a place where you try on fancy clothes and act like you are going to buy them.

Jan Barrick, my roommate and friend of many years, just called her husband in Oklahoma City to "check in." They have just been married two years instead of thirty-six like Louis and me so she "checks in" often. Jan is a very slow dresser, so I went downstairs to reserve the limo and stop by the bar for a gin and tonic. I'm so glad I did.

Rychee (pronounced Rickey) Cole waited on me—a really pretty girl about thirty years old. The phone rang after she'd served me, and she spoke quickly and angrily to somebody.

"Bad times?" inquires me, of course.

"Yes," says she, "but I try to keep my mind set on better things."

"What's the trouble?" I ask, and I really want to know. You know me, I'm just like you in that regard.

"Well . . ." and the dam burst. "They won't ever let us know ahead of time when we are working next week, and I have a little boy, and he has a birthday, and I'm planning a party and all this is giving me a headache! I could wait on my customers better if I didn't have a hurtin' head!"

"Have you worked here long?" I ask.

"Oh, no. I'm a fourth-grade teacher in the fall and spring, but I make more money working here."

Hummm, thinks I. A story, a story.

"How old is your son and what kind of party are you going to have?" my inquiring mind wants to know. I am guessing cake and ice cream and pin-the-tail on the donkey.

"Amir's going to be five, and we've invited twenty kids."

"Twenty five-year-olds?" I say amazed.

"Well, no, they are all ages from six months to fifteen. Amir has lots of friends. Amir's daddy is going to fry chicken and he's making potato salad and leafy green salad. Amir loves lettuce. It's going to be a good old-fashioned picnic."

"I think it's great that Amir's daddy is doing all that work," I say.

"Yes, and he gave me sixty dollars for the prizes."

The kid is gonna be five. "Sixty dollars? Good grief! What kind of prizes?"

She's wiping the counter clean as she says, "Oh, Power Rangers, stuff like that for the little ones, and Nikes for the big ones."

"Nikes??" says I. "You mean, as in shoes?"

"Amir's daddy says he can get them for us wholesale. He works at a shoe store."

"Hit me again," says I, draining my glass and wondering whatever happened to little hats and balloons.

Molly

"Bringing in the Sheaves."

Billie, my dear sister,

Obviously, I am trying to "soften you up" with such an address. It's because I think you may not believe the story. Believe it. It's true. For somebody somewhere, at least.

It is 4:30 A.M. L.A. time and I am sitting at the biggest desk I have ever seen in the lobby of the biggest hotel I have ever seen thinking that I really need a laptop computer because my handwriting is so bad and I'm having to write this BY HAND on hotel stationery. But I can't even do a regular computer, so how could I do a laptop?

Can you believe that the people in California are just as shiftless and lazy as some people I know in Oklahoma? It is already 4:40 A.M. and nobody but me is awake.

I realize that there is a two-hour difference and it is really 2:20 Oklahoma time, but it looks like some of them would be letting their cats out now, which is what I would be doing were I in Norman, Oklahoma, where things are NORMAL.

As it is, I am in the lobby of the hotel (Jan is sleeping soundly, an advantage of being young!) where there is a beautiful grand piano, and lucky for me, it is not locked. So I sit down and play "Bringing in the Sheaves," the chorus only, three times. I had nine years of piano lessons under the stern hand of Kate Johnson in Apache, Oklahoma, and now I can play "Bringing in the Sheaves," chorus only.

That's it.

That's all I can play.

Nine years.

Can you believe that? As well as you know me, I'm sure you can.

Oh, wait! I forgot! I can also play the first eight measures of "The Hungarian Rhapsody IV" . . . or maybe III or II. I'm not as good at H. R. IV as I am at "Bringing in the Sheaves" as you might have guessed. It goes "Ti dum, ti, dum. Ta da da dum, ti dum!" You do recognize it, don't you? That's as far as I ever got.

The only other person awake in this hotel is a guy named Dane who works for Edward D. Jones and is from . . . you guessed it . . . Bentonville, Arkansas. He is wandering around the lobby listening to my playing "Bringing in the Sheaves" and wishing he were home in Arkansas. He is the broker for a guy named David Glass who is the CEO for . . . right again . . . Wal-Mart.

If you don't believe this, consider that there is no way in God's world that I would know who is the CEO of Wal-Mart. Or who his broker is. Check it out and decide whether I make up things or not!

Old Dave and I got to be good friends and he's gonna find out why Wal-Mart is not carrying your book.

As our friend Betsy Hailey often says, "To be continued."

Molly

"Can't you just add a few drops of spinach juice?"

August 15, 1996

Dear Billie,

I hope you have had your breakfast, because this is a letter about blood. There's no gore involved, however, just blood. And Sister, who frequently gives it. Now, I am not against donating blood. I do it myself from time to time because I have A negative and that is kind of rare. As a matter of fact, ours was a rare family because all four of us—Mama, Daddy, Sister, and I—all have (or had) A negative blood. Statistically that's amazing, but we were a pretty amazing bunch, says she modestly.

49

Anyway, Sister, who has always been strange, loves to give blood. Sometimes she is barely able to wait until the appropriate number of days have passed. Long Fourth of July weekends or other holiday blood drives are her specialty. Now I accuse her of giving so often just because she likes the free orange juice and cookie, but she denies it. Maybe she's a vampire in reverse.

Well, when she went to donate in response to the Red Cross plea yesterday, she was in for a shock.

"No, Mrs. Vineyard," said the prim and proper, heavy-bottomed, white-starched nurse who was checking Sister's computer report and rejecting her as a blood donor. "We can't take your blood today. You are low on iron. You only register thirty-six and you need to be at least thirty-eight."

Sister was enraged. And humiliated.

"Can't you just take my blood, add a few drops of spinach juice, and shake the bag real well?" Sister says she asked Miss Prim, and I am certain she was whining when she said it. She really wanted that cookie and orange juice.

Are you sure you want to be kin to us? What type blood do you have?

Love,
Molly

"Well, I've been robbed!"

August 31, 1996

Dear Billie,

Well, it finally happened. My dear sweet mother-in-law, whom I love as much as I loved my mother, got robbed today.

She was so pleased.

Mattie will be eighty-five years old on October 16. She has lived alone since Louis' father died seven years ago. She stayed in their house in Anadarko for three years, then moved to Norman at our insistence. Louis is an only. In the entire thirty-six years Louis and I have been married, she has asked me for help twice. That was when she had her two cataract operations last year. I drove her to the hospital at 6:30 A.M., waited while the surgery was performed, and took her to Denny's for breakfast at 11:00 afterwards. She's a wonder.

I had to do the surgery trips because "Louis works," she explained. I, being self-employed, do not "work" in the same manner that he works, although she is in great admiration of what I have done with my business. However, being self-employed, I do not have a boss who might ask where I was going. Cataract surgery, like everything else in Mattie's life, is a very private affair. Think of what Louis' boss at Kerr-McGee could do with that kind of information.

Better not risk it.

Mattie had to wait eighty-five and one-half years to get robbed. She knew it was going to happen. She talked about it often. And like the story about the guy who went to the storm cellar every time a cloud appeared for years and was pleased when he finally came out to find his entire house blown away, Mattie called me at work yesterday to say triumphantly, "Well, I've been robbed. I knew it was bound to happen someday. And this is the day!"

She sounded a lot like Shannon Miller when she told the world that she had trained her entire life for just this moment. The gold medal at last! Mattie's lifelong distrust of humanity had finally paid off.

"Mattie!" I shouted into the phone, "Are you all right? Did you get hurt? Where did this happen?" I had picked her up that very morning about 9:00, driven her to the city for a follow up on the cataract surgery, had lunch, and taken her home. The phone call came about fifteen minutes after I had seen her to her door.

"Oh, I'm fine," says she. "I don't think they took anything. I think maybe I interrupted them."

"You mean they might still be in the house?" I was really wild. "Go outside immediately. Wait for me in the front yard. I'll be right there!"

And I was. And she was. Right in the front yard, smiling

broadly. "I did what you told me to do," says she. "But I think they had left already. I don't think they got anything."

"But how do you know that somebody was in your house?" I pressed, thinking that perhaps the day had been a little boring and maybe she needed a little excitement although she had never exhibited those tendencies before. She is, after all, eighty-four.

"Well, the chair in my bedroom had been moved across the rug. And the desk drawer was left open half an inch," she mused. The eye surgery was certainly successful.

"It's just like one of those Miss Marple stories, isn't it?" she questioned happily.

I mentally returned to my dull day/excitement theory.

But when we went in, the chair had indeed been dragged across the floor, the desk drawer was open a bit (Mattie never leaves anything open) and further search turned up an empty billfold inside a bank bag in the desk drawer.

"Well, they got Lyle's last $30," she observed.

Lyle was my father-in-law.

"Pop's money?" I say. "But he's been dead seven years."

"Well, they gave me his billfold at the hospital after he died, and it had $30 in it. I never saw the need to empty it. If I had ever needed his money, I knew where it was."

Oh, my.

"But I bet they didn't get the money in that 7-Up can you gave me," she said heading for the closet.

Knowing her distrust and fears, some years ago I had purchased a wonderful fail-safe safe of sorts, a fake 7-Up can which had a lid that screwed on and was empty inside. The idea was that you stuffed your cash inside, screwed the perfectly shaped lid back on, popped the can in the frig among other cans of Coke, Pepsi, etc., and even the most astute burglar would not think to look there.

Trying to figure out why she was headed for the closet rather than the refrigerator, I said, "Yep, I bet you fooled them big time with that fake 7-Up can!"

"You are right," said Mattie, emerging from the walk-in closet with a bundle of towels. "It's still here!" And she carefully unwrapped towel after towel until she came to the tricky 7-Up can bank. She had hidden it well. In the closet. Under the towels. Those robbers would have never figured that out. I was sure glad we had interrupted them.

Love,
Molly

"You don't have to stay in the lines . . ."

September 6, 1996

Dear Billie,

You have no doubt noticed that I am by nature a pretty upbeat, positive person, an optimistic soul who always thinks the sun is about to burst through even during very long dry spells, right?

That's why I was very surprised, puzzled, more than a little confused this morning when I woke up in a blue funk that enveloped my entire body, head, and heart.

"Your children are well," I say to myself. "Your husband is well. You are well. Almost everybody I know and love is reasonably well at this moment in time. (Wellness is right at the top of my "Be thankful for" list these days.) Most of the bills are paid, nothing which is supposed to spin has stopped doing so . . . washer, dryer, dishwasher. No cavities, no bunions, not even a slight blister to mar my day. What was it?

Still in my nightshirt, the one emblazoned "I don't do mornings!" I pulled on gray socks to match my mood, run-down walking shoes to match my body, and I headed for the door. "Fresh air, fresh outlook," I repeated in time to my steps.

No luck.

There was something missing. Something wrong. Something that I used to have that I didn't have anymore. My mind searched for it, kind of like your tongue looked for the missing tooth when you were six. September air brushed my cheeks as I kicked into high walking gear. The sun was just starting to crawl its way over the horizon. As old Sol began his daily push ups, the navy night sky began a technicolor tango. Those wonderful beautiful colors—Cherub Pink, Frank Sinatra Blue. Suddenly, it struck me! I knew what I needed, what would really, really make me happy.

A box of Crayola crayons. A brand new 48-colors-with-a-sharpener-on-the-back box of Crayola crayons.

School was about to start, and I didn't have new colors. Remember how they smelled? Remember how wonderfully sharp and pointy they were? Remember when not a single one of your crayons had been broken?

Even though I have a real bone to pick with Sam Walton, he is the only Crayola game in town at 5:30 A.M. So I raced myself back home, grabbed my car keys, threw the three cats off the top of the Winkler, and roared off to Wal-Mart.

I had the whole Back to School department to myself (which shows what kind of wimps we have in our schools these days, sound asleep at 5:30 A.M.).

Have you bought any Crayola crayons lately? They have changed all kinds of things . . . colors, box sizes, prices. When I was a school girl there were three choices: a box of six fat crayons for babies, which nobody but Thomas Jones who wet his pants in the second grade would be caught dead with; a twelve-crayon box, which the kids over the track saved all summer for; and the great big wonderful 48 Crayola, which was, of course, what I always had and what I bought this morning. Only a really decadent person would buy a box with more than 48 crayons.

Now the book was a much bigger problem. Not being a fan of either Barney or Pocahontas, my choices were severely limited. I spent a long time leafing through bears, rabbits, and other riffraff, when I suddenly found the "You Don't Have to Stay in the Lines Coloring Book." With a happy hoop, I flipped it open and it was blank, completely blank! What a joy. What a smart, smart coloring book company.

I bought one for me and another one for Thomas Jones. To go with the crayons I had already picked up for him.

I can't be the only one who feels this way.
I'll bet Thomas Jones does, too.

Love,
Molly

"An optimist doesn't shake the handle."

September 20, 1996

Dear Sister Billie,

Today I need to tell you about the house. The house is very important to our history, Sister's and mine. This is the house we grew up in. It was built the summer and fall of 1925. I have a letter from my father to my mother (he, too was a compulsive letter writer; he wrote me every day my freshman year of college) dated July 13, 1925. The letter says, "They dug the basement for our house today." In an odd coincidence of dates, my birthday would occur thirteen years later on July 13. We have an old red and white suitcase filled with ninety-three letters tied with thin blue ribbons, quite faded now, which he sent to Mama when they were courting. They are filled with wonderful declarations of love and detailed descriptions of house construction.

They lived in that house for forty-nine years, four months, and twenty-one days, that Jewish letter writer and his thirteen years younger Irish Baptist flapper. And then Daddy died. And Mama went right on living there for ten more years. Lilly Maude West Levite and her memories. She died on Christmas Eve of 1985.

I sold that house on a hot August day in 1986. And when we were finished at the bank with things like loans and abstracts I went home for the last time. Sister couldn't bear to go with me. If it were now, she could, but in 1986 she was too young. Back then, I was the big sister. Now she is.

When I rolled into that driveway, I was amazed at how wide it was . . . much wider than I remembered it to be. As a sixteen-year-old, I had backed out of that driveway, cut to the left, and driven forward into the Caldwells' driveway next door until the water gauge turned red. July birthdays are hard on engines.

August days are hard on hearts. I opened the car door slowly, got out, and walked around the corner of the house to the back door. The very old key to the very old door did not stick. I was hoping it would.

I walked through the back porch and the kitchen, trying not to see the emptiness. I entered the enormous cavern which was the living room/dining area. It wasn't really that big; it just looked that way because it was empty for the first time in sixty-one years. All that was left were the window seats.

You remember window seats, don't you? Those neat storage chests with hinged tops on them? They were the fashion in 1925, and there were two of them in our house. If we had only known each other when we were little, we could have played hide-and-go seek there, you and Sister and I.

They looked very much alike, those two window boxes. But we who lived there knew that the one on the north was by far the better one because it had a hole drilled to the outside for the telephone wire to run through. With careful breathing, you could stay in there a very long time and not smother.

"You could maybe even stay in there a hundred years and not run out of air," Sister told me once when we were little.

I took one look at that north window seat and walked straight to it. I got in and started to close the lid. Sister had said you could hide in there maybe a hundred years and not die. She's six and a half years older than me, remember, and I always thought she knew important things like that.

The lid wouldn't close.

That lid I had trusted for so long to hide me would not close.

I was too big.

So I just sat there in that window seat and cried.

56

After a while I got tired of crying, so I started to remember.

I remembered Christmas trees that sat in the corner right next to the window seat. Always in the same spot. I remembered a tiny little Santa light bulb which we hung from a piece of green thread when it burned out, as all lights do.

We could not bear to part with that Santa light bulb, Sister and I, so we tied that piece of green thread to it and hung it for an ornament.

It was our favorite one. I wondered where it was.

By the time my mind reached the doll house which was hidden under Daddy's big brown overcoat at the back of the tree, the doll house I thought wasn't there at all until the BIG FLOURISH, I had to stop remembering or I would smother in spite of what Sister had told me.

So I climbed out.

And I walked to the back door.

I opened it and walked outside into the hot, stifling August air.

I closed the door and locked it behind me.

"An optimist closes the door, locks it, and doesn't shake the handle to see if the lock really worked," Daddy told me once when I was about twelve, and we were closing the store for the night. "A pessimist," he went on, "jiggles the handle to see if the lock has held."

As I heard that lock click shut behind me, I heard those words as clearly as I had when Daddy said them the first time. I did not rattle the handle.

I climbed into my car, started the engine, and began to back out. For some reason, that driveway seemed much, much narrower than it had been when I had driven in.

Do you suppose that closing a book is easier than opening it because the spine has been bent so much? I wonder.

Love,
Molly

The four rules . . .

October 2, 1996

Dear Billie,

In order that you really understand me, you need to understand Louis, whose mother gave him four rules to follow the day he started first grade. She told him:

1. Do not drink or eat after anyone else. Ever.
2. If you have to have a B.M. at school, cover the toilet seat with toilet paper.
3. Remember where you hang your cap and jacket so you can find them later.
4. Never have anything to do with any child named Larue.

We have been married for thirty-six years, but I only found out about the four rules last week. I was packing our two Thermos jugs of water to take to the game. They are exactly alike. And both filled with cold water. We do not take two because we need that much water. We take two because Louis will not drink after me. He does all kinds of other things to, for, and with my mouth, but he has never—repeat never—eaten or drunk after me. See rule number 1 above.

Not knowing about rule number one as I poured the water, I said, "You know, it has always puzzled me that you joyfully do all sorts of interesting things to all parts of my body including my mouth, but you won't drink after me. Why is that?"

"My mother told me not to," he replied simply. "It was the first of her four rules."

I was amazed and intrigued. "Four rules? What four rules?"

"The four rules she gave me the day I started first grade. Didn't your mother give you rules?" he asked with narrowed eyes and more than a hint of suspicion in his voice.

"Let me think," I replied, trying frantically to make up some rules and get my poor dead Mama off the hook. My mama had no rules. And for once I had trouble trying to make some up. "You tell me yours first," I said, trying to buy some time.

He then repeated the rules listed above.

It was number four, of course, that grabbed my attention.

"Never have anything to do with any child named Larue? What did that mean? Who were the Larues? Why did she single them out?"

"I started school in La Crosse, Wisconsin," he explained as if to a slow learning child. "There was a big French population there at that time and most of them were what my farm girl, Missouri mother thought of as 'white trash.' The Larue family was particularly trashy," he said simply. "So I was not to have anything to do with them."

"That's it?" I asked in amazement. "Your mother said for you not to have anything to do with them, so you didn't?"

"That's right," says Mama's little boy with pride.

"I would have asked them home to supper the first night just to see what my Mama would do," I told him.

"I'll bet you would have," says Louis. "And Marie Yvette would have wet her pants at your kitchen table."

"Wet her pants?"

"Yes," Louis answered, shifting into the patience-of-Job voice he often uses with me. "You see, my mother knew best when she told me not to have anything to do with any child named Larue. In the first grade, you expect a certain amount of pants wetting in some of the children, Mother had told me. Some children are frightened of new situations. But Marie Yvette sat right at her desk, coloring, and wet her pants. Sitting down. At her desk. The teacher heard the tinkling sound, looked up, and said, 'You, you Larue girl. Go home.' So you see, my mother was right!

I wonder what my life would have been like if I had married one of Marie Yvette's brothers? What do you think?

Love,
Molly

I do mine for bison.

November 16, 1996

Hello!

I am very sorry I woke you up this morning, but those who sleep until 5:00 A.M. on a Saturday should expect such things.

It's Oklahoma history time! I used to teach Oklahoma history; did you know that? Don't you find that frightening? I mean, Abe Lincoln said, "History is not history unless it is true." And I have been known to hold the truth lightly from time to time. But only on Thursdays. And this is Saturday.

Oklahoma became a state on November 16, 1907. Teddy Roosevelt was president of the United States at that time. He had visited Oklahoma and had met with Quanah Parker, the last chief of the Comanches. Quanah Parker told the president how sad the Indians were that there were no longer any buffalo in what was to become the great state of Oklahoma.

This gave Teddy Roosevelt an idea. He arranged for fifteen buffalo to be shipped from the Bronx Zoo in New York to the Wildlife Refuge in the Wichita Mountains near Lawton. They were shipped by train. In each city they passed, all the people came out to see the buffalo which were going to live in the brand new state of Oklahoma. Many of those people had never even seen a buffalo except in pictures in books. The buffalo got pretty nasty from time to time and kicked out the slats of the train.

When the train arrived in Cache, Oklahoma Territory, the buffalo were unloaded from the boxcar which had been fixed especially for them. This was in October of 1907. Some of the buffalo were expecting babies, so they were gently loaded into crates and taken to an enclosed area in the Wichita Mountains, where they were fed and cared for that first winter. Legend has it that the first baby buffalo was born on statehood day, November 16, 1907. The little girl buffalo was named OKLAHOMA!

Now you know why I wrote a book called *The Buffalo in the Mall*. Those Bronx Zoo buffalo descendants have never been to a mall, and I think that was discriminatory. So if they read my book, they will be there in their minds. And that's what counts. You do yours for people. I do mine for bison.

This is not one of my better letters because a great deal of it is true and truth is not nearly as much fun to write.

Has Jay Leno called yet? I bet you were wide awake and perky when he did because of me. He will call you one of these days, you know!

Molly

It's times like these that it's nice to be a girl.

November 24, 1996

Dear Billie,

Well, I just got in from my morning two-mile walk wherein I almost fell over in the street and got run over by a garbage truck because I was laughing so hard at Sister's story of the day.

People often say, "What in the world could you have to say to your sister every day?" To which I reply, "Do you have a sister?" because I can't imagine why they would ask such a question since we never get it all said. That's why we adopted you, so you could have two people who would listen.

Anyway, on a previous tape from me to her I had extolled the virtues of wetting in one's panties in public. On purpose. Sometimes, such an act is not only necessary, but also downright exhilarating. "Necessity is the mother of" or something like that. One day in late September I had just finished a grueling day of booth work at Encyclomedia, that neat book convention the State Department of Education has every year. You signed for me there once, I believe. Anyway, it's lucrative, but a killer on the feet. And the bladder.

You may recall that Encyclomedia is held at the Myriad in Oklahoma City, which is not far from Louis' office. He had dropped me off that morning and said he'd pick me up on the south corner of the building at 5:00. It was now 5:00. I didn't realize how bad I needed to go until the door was slamming behind me, and it was then that I realized that it was one of those fire exits that doesn't have an outside handle. It was miles to the front entrance, and if I attempted to reach it, I would miss Louis.

Well, I squirmed for a minute or two and then realized I was going to be in real agony during the long, thirty-minute ride to Norman. I had on a pair of shoes I am really attached to because they don't hurt, and I didn't want to ruin them. So I stepped primly onto a patch of grass, removed my shoes, smiled at the passing cars, and wet for all I was worth. It's times like these that it's nice to be a girl. A boy would have gotten his skirt all wet, don't you think?

Until I did it in full view of the many passing cars, I didn't know what fun public urination could be. Luckily I had a pack of tissues in my purse, so when I finished, I demurely wiped my feet as best I could under the circumstances. I could shower when I got home.

I waited a few minutes, thinking how glad I was that Louis was late, and then stepped back into my shoes and onto the sidewalk. Louis came, I got in the pickup and had a very comfortable ride back home.

Have I ever told you that I never wear perfume because Louis has absolutely no sense of smell at all? It's true. He doesn't. And there have been many, many times in our marriage that this was of great advantage to me.

This was one of them.

Anyway, back to Sister's tape today, and why I found it so funny. Not to be outdone by me, she had gone out into her backyard, stood in the flower bed, and wet her pants. With no one, not even a garbage man, watching. Now I ask you, what kind of pants-wetting is that? And here is the real ripper . . . she was embarrassed. Very embarrassed.

I've told you before she is strange. Very strange. And probably not really my blood sister. I've often suspected that a band of gypsies might have stolen me and left me on the Levite doorstep in Apache. I am probably really a Larue.

Love,
Molly

Pray without ceasing.

November 26, 1996

Dear Billie,

Since we were both teachers, and we were talking on the phone yesterday about the influence we might or might not have on our students, I decided to write you about the teacher who had the most profound influence on my life.

Strangely enough, or perhaps not strangely at all now that I think of it, the most lasting influence a teacher had on my life came not from a school teacher, but from a Sunday school teacher. Maybe lessons learned on Sunday soak in deeper, do you think?

She had no children of her own, this Sunday lady in my life. Perhaps that is why she prepared so carefully for us. I'm not sure of this, but I don't think most Sunday school teachers take their jobs as seriously as Mrs. Hazel Myers did, but then again, perhaps they do. I hope so. She taught at the First Christian Church in Apache. You remember that my Jewish father married Baptist Mama, who raised Sister and me in the First Christian Church because that was where her friends went. We Levites were quite ecumenical.

I'm sure we were a noisy, rambunctious bunch: Pauline and Paul (brother and sister), Sue (my best friend), Carol Ann, Paula, Nelda Jo (I'm sure I am forgetting someone), but fifty years ripped from the calendar have not dimmed my memory of Mrs. Myers and her Sunday school class.

She got us at just the right time—sixth, seventh, and eighth grades, a time when we were really beginning to form our opinions, ask our many questions, and establish our soon-to-be adult relationship with God. Her God was down to earth and matter of fact. Her versions of the Bible were concrete.

She explained that Jesus was able to feed the multitudes not by breaking the bread over and over with a magician's touch, but by gently persuading the irritable and weary crowd to share what they had brought with their neighbors who had not brought anything. A much greater miracle than magic, this ability to get selfish people to share. She explained that the "needle's eye" was the name of the small low gate which admitted the camel-riding stranger into the old walled cities. Therefore, it was "harder for a camel to go through the eye of a needle than it was for a rich man to enter the Kingdom of God" because man had to humble himself on his knees in order to enter the gate to the city.

But most important of all, Mrs. Myers taught us to pray. "Pray without ceasing." I have read that the best definition of the word "normal" is "what you are used to." My Jewish father went into the closet to say his prayers each night. My Christian mother prayed mostly when things were burning. Mrs. Myers was big on "pray without ceasing."

"Prayer is as necessary for your spiritual life as air is for your natural life," she said over and over and over again.

And we believed her. And we prayed. Without ceasing.

What a wonderful teacher she was!

Since it's Thanksgiving, I'll be thankful for Mrs. Myers!

Molly

Molly—

Let me provide some insight to the condition I'm in just now—I first made out this check to "Language of Apache." Then, I addressed an envelope to 113 Hal Linden Drive. (Wasn't Hal Linden the star of <u>Barney Miller</u>?) But I'm beginning to settle down now. (Those anxiety pills work miracles, don't they, Milly?) I'm down to the loose ends on the book—acknowledgments, dedication and permissions—then it's on to Christmas. Guess it's time to shop—agonizing over choices, guilt that comes with being a cheapskate, self-pity—whining—carrying the burden without assistance from spouse. Ain't the holidays fun?

Love you,
Buffy

He trusts no one.

December 2, 1996

Dear Billie,

First of all, let me assure you that I did NOT open the Christmas present Louis bought me over the weekend and hid behind the quilts because I was dying to know what was in it. I opened it because I was seriously considering cutting off my long raven-black hair and selling it to buy him a watch fob and I wanted to be sure he had not hocked the watch his grandfather gave him years ago. Besides that, those quilts are the obvious place someone of Louis' limited imagination would pick; to have not looked there would have been strange. I look there every day all year long, just in case there is some gift-giving occasion I might have forgotten.

Anyway, it took me an awful long time to open that silver-and-blue box in a way that he could not tell it had been opened. He will check it out tonight. And every night between now and Christmas Eve, I might add. The man trusts no one.

Louis still sees me as a size 10.

January 1, 1997

Happy New Year!

I just found this unfinished Christmas Letts Letter that needs finishing, but right now I'm busy starting the New Year, so I'll just pop in what I had done with the firm resolve to finish it when I have time.

The box held boots, wonderful, perfect-fitting black leather boots, so I did not have to take them back and exchange them for a bigger size, as I might have had to do if it had been a dress. Louis, God bless him, still sees me as a size 10 with a 23-inch waist. I was size 10 when we married. I lied about the

65

23-inch waist. And lucky for me, he never took a tape measure to me.

May your '97 be filled with lots of royalty checks and a finished manuscript!

Love,
Molly

Mother of a ship launcher.

January 20, 1997

Dear Billie,

Louis came home with the most amazing news today!

Ginger, our red-haired computer person daughter, gets to launch a ship. In March. In Japan. IN PERSON.

Isn't that amazing? Especially since Louis is neither an admiral nor the president of the United States. I thought only movie stars and Margaret Truman launched ships, and here I'm about to become the mother of a ship launcher.

Here's how it all came about. Louis deals with a Japanese company through his job at Kerr-McGee. The company ships cargo from Japan to the U.S. and a lot of other places, too. It is their custom to have a single female whose father works for the company to launch the ship which is to receive the first shipment on its maiden voyage. This female must herself be a "maiden," as in single. Kerr-McGee's Mobile plant gets the first shipment, and Ginger gets to crack the champagne!

To make it even more interesting for the Japanese, Ginger is a redhead with beautiful long tresses. There aren't a lot of those in Japan. Or in Singapore, either, I'd guess. Have you all gone to visit Shawn since he moved to Singapore? I've been looking at maps and globes a lot lately, and all of those places are sure a long way from Norman and Durant, America.

Louis gets to go with her, and I'm really glad as they will have a neat father-daughter time. I'll keep an eye on the cats, the shop, and Mattie. Actually, she'll be keeping an eye on us, I imagine.

"I've never been
to Salt Lake City."

January 29, 1997

Dear Billie,

Just so you won't think I'm the only one in my family that crazy things happen to . . .

My cute twenty-six-year-old redhead and her boyfriend were invited to a Super Bowl party last Sunday. It was being held at the home of a couple in Dallas (Ginger lives in Irving) who were friends of Ginger's young man. Ginger had never met these folks. When they arrived, Gin spied a throw on the couch which depicted historical events in Ponca City, and upon inquiry she found that the hostess was an Okie also.

When Gin told the couple of her own Oklahoma roots, the hostess exclaimed, "You're from Norman! We have another friend who is coming who is from Norman! His name is Kurt DePriest."

Ginger was happily surprised by this news because Kurt had been a classmate of hers. In fact, he had been the first little boy to give her a Valentine way back when they were in the first grade together at Cleveland Elementary School twenty some years ago. They had had quite a puppy love crush on each other, but Kurt had moved away the next summer and she had never seen or heard of him again. But one does not forget one's first love. The hostess could not wait to reunite them.

By the time Kurt and his fiancée arrived, the party was in full swing, and the TV was blaring the football game.

The hostess, who had been eagerly awaiting the big moment when she could renew an old acquaintance, grabbed Ginger by the hand, presented her to Kurt and his girl, saying with a flourish, "Kurt, this is Ginger! She's from Norman!"

Due to the noise and confusion, the fiancée thought she said, "This is Ginger! She's a Mormon!"

So when Kurt responded quite loudly, "Oh, my God! This is unbelievable! You can't be!" the fiancée thought that this man she was going to marry soon was questioning this poor strange redhaired woman's religious affiliation.

"Honey," she interjects, totally humiliated, "please!"

"I can't believe it!" Kurt continues, taking Ginger's hands and stepping back to inspect her better. "Look at her!" he commands his fiancée. "A pretty girl like this! Can you believe it?"

The poor fiancée, still thinking her guy is having a hissy fit because the lovely Ginger is a Mormon, attempts to apologize for his boorish behavior.

"I don't know what has come over him," she says to Ginger. "He is normally quite tolerant. We both think Salt Lake is a lovely city," she adds lamely, ". . . all those beautiful temples . . ."

Ginger, who hasn't a clue as to what the woman is talking about, says, "Oh, I'm pretty tolerant myself, but I've never been to Salt Lake City."

Edward Albee would have loved it, don't you think?

Love,
Molly

"Is there a cash award?"

February 2, 1997

Dear Billie,

I am so glad that Howard Starks' book is a finalist for the Oklahoma Book Award, too! I could hear you squealing clear up here in Norman when you found out. He's a fine poet and the book itself is a real labor of love on the part of the printer. Both my son and my daughter were properly impressed when I called them to tell them that my book was a finalist. But then there is Mattie. I know what she will say—believe me, I know. Mattie, my beloved mother-in-law (and you know that I mean that sincerely; I love her), will say, "Now what exactly does this mean?"

And I will say, "Oh, Mattie, it is wonderful! It is a great honor!"

And she will say, "Yes, but what does it really mean? Is there a cash award?"

"Well, no, but they hang a nice medal on a lovely velvet ribbon around your neck."

"I've never liked velvet as well as grosgrain," she'll say. "Will President Clinton present the award to you?" she'll ask sweetly without looking up from her plate. (We'll be eating lunch when this conversation transpires.)

"Well, no, but the governor might be there," I'll say defensively.

"I didn't vote for him," she'll reply. "If President Clinton presented it, you would get to fly, expenses paid, to Washington, D.C., for a week and get to tour the White House and sleep in Lincoln's bed. I didn't vote for him either."

"I really prefer my own mattress," I'll say through my teeth.

"Will you appear on any national television programs? If so, I'll call my sister Helen's rest home and have them install cable so she can watch you."

"Well, no," I'll say. "Pass the cabbage, please." But they will probably put an article in *The Daily Oklahoman* and maybe even *The Tulsa World*. I know *The Apache News* will feature it."

"I bet they will all spell our name wrong," she'll say with a sigh. "They always do ... Griffin or Griffith, they always spell it wrong. Do you want more cabbage? I don't. It always repeats on me, but you go ahead. Maybe next year you'll be nominated for something really nice, dear. You must keep trying."

I do love her.

I really do.

"No, no more cabbage," I'll say. "Cabbage repeats on me, too."

Love,
Molly

"Ya gotta have a gimmick!"

February 15, 1997

Dear Billie,

Being from a big city like Tulsa, you may not know anything about a school organization called FFA—Future Farmers of America. In Apache, it ruled the roost (awful visual images intentional) as far as school clubs go. Any boy who was anybody belonged to FFA and showed his hogs with pride. Even the town kids like my best friend Paul, who was destined to become a radiologist, was a member of FFA. Paul joined so he could have the thrill of going through the initiation which consisted of things like having to eat bananas from a bedpan full of an unidentifiable liquid while blindfolded after carefully being made to feel that the container was indeed a slop jar. Neat stuff like that.

(I was one of a select few females in the town who got to witness the initiation because I was FFA queen one year, but that is another story entirely.)

Anyway, in order to counteract this male-only, sexist organization which was founded on the premise that girls could not be farmers and therefore were not allowed membership in Future Farmers of America, some far-sighted home economics teacher got the idea of establishing FHA, which of course stood for Future Homemakers of America.

I, of course, was a proud, card-carrying member of FHA.

This organization had local clubs, district clubs, and also a tremendous state organization which had a great convention in Oklahoma City every year. Going to that convention was one of the highlights of my young life. We shopped for months for the perfect outfit to wear complete with two-and-a-half-inch high heels. Having the perfect outfit was a big part of being the perfect homemaker. We walked the streets of Oklahoma City in those high heels until our feet were killing us. Then we went to the Convention Center for the evening performance, which was always some really stunning musical performance by somebody really famous like Dick Hames. During the program we took our shoes off, our feet swelled, and we had to walk back to the school buses barefoot. Most of us had already taken off our nylon hose on the way up Oklahoma City to put them over our face and heads so we could sit on the back seat of the school bus and look out the window. We scared the devil out of the drivers of the cars behind the bus.

We were Future Homemakers and damn proud of it.

Anyway, the reason I have to tell you this is that I, your unassuming, rather quiet and reserved friend, was once elected district vice president of the Future Homemakers of America with a campaign speech which was climaxed by my taking my dress off and standing on my head.

I was fifteen at the time.

I guess I had watched *Gypsy* one too many times and decided that, in order to win, "Ya gotta have a gimmick!"

I have always been able to stand on my head . . . still can as a matter of fact . . . and it always seemed to garner votes of one kind or another. So when I traveled to the district convention in Bowlegs, I had on my acrobatic costume under my church dress. The costume was pink, glowed in the dark, and had "MOLLY" emblazoned across the top in gold sequins. The dress was mauve.

The other girl running for district vice president was one of two people I knew in my youth who wore braces. And glasses. And had very long, very stringy, quite unkempt hair. And she could never have stood on her head in a million years.

She didn't have a prayer.

I wish I were making this up.

But I'm not.

I won.

Love,
Molly

February 22, 1997

Dear Billie,

As I have told you before, my father was a strong, positive influence on my life. Although he has been gone from this
plane for twenty-two years, his guidance and advice still echo
in my mind when times get tough. When I use his tools—his
hammer, his saw, plane—I feel his blood coursing through my
veins and am strengthened. I thought of him this morning
when I went to check the buds on our pear tree, which seems
to have fooled itself into believing it is spring. Such mistakes
can cost one one's life, you know. Trees conjure my father's face.

When I was six and ready to enter the hallowed halls of
learning (first grade of Apache Elementary School), Daddy
walked me over to the school playground one hot, dusty
August day and sat with me under the comforting shade of an
enormous old elm tree. Actually, there were four trees set in
the shape of a somewhat irregular baseball diamond. I sat in
the middle, and he patted the trunk of the tallest of the four.

"This is your tree," he told me as he gently pried a tiny
piece of bark from the old trunk and placed it in my hand. "I
planted it the spring of 1904. I was ten years old at the time
and had no idea that I was planting it for you to play under
someday."

He was forty-five when I was born, this Johnny Appleseed
of mine, the age of many of my friends' grandfathers. Had I
been old enough to add my six years to his forty-five and sub-
tract the difference I would have been quite impressed to be
the owner and beneficiary of a tree that was forty-one years
old. But at the age of six I only knew that it was very wonderful to be the owner of such a big tree. The roots went out
in all directions and were worn bare by generations of children
who had played there. Those roots seemed to form the rooms
of a house, rooms with invisible walls that could keep out any
silly boy who wanted to interrupt things the way silly boys
always did when I was six.

"Apache was new," Daddy went on, "and so was the school. This old playground was bare by the time they finished laying out the town. The first Arbor Day, our teachers marched us all down to Cache Creek, where each one of us dug up a sapling, wrapped it in burlap, and drug it back to the school yard. Then each of us had the task of digging a hole, planting our tree, and keeping it watered." He patted his tree again.

"Lot of those trees died, but mine was a strong little sapling, and here she is all these years later waiting to watch you play." The sunlight burst through the leaves about that time and the wind picked up a bit.

"But how do you know that this one was yours?" I wanted to know.

"Oh, I know," Daddy replied. "I watched it grow every day for years and years. I wouldn't get my tree mixed up with anybody else's tree, any more than I would get you mixed up with any other little girl in the world."

I certainly knew that to be true. As was everything else my Daddy told me. I clearly remember that day when I was six. It was the first inkling I had that something I did might be remembered for a long, long time.

Love,
Molly

. . . blowing my nose on the sheets . . .

March 15, 1997

Dear Billie,

Well, I put Louis on the plane this morning at 6:00 A.M. for Japan. Actually he was headed for Dallas first, where he would link up with Ginger, and they would fly the friendly skies to Japan where they would arrive a day after they had left. They will return the day before they leave. Or vice versa

73

as there is an eleven-or twelve-hour time difference as you know since one of your kids lives there. I have a theory that if you jumped from one plane to another from those places, you would never grow old, just like in the field of dreams, where you would stay twenty-one in a baseball game that never ends.

I wish I had taken up baseball.

Anyway, I am now alone for two weeks. As always, when Louis leaves for two weeks (this used to happen often when he was in the Army Reserve . . . you don't think he has that burr haircut for nothing, do you?) the first thing I do is make a list of things I am going to do while he is gone: 1. lose ten pounds (the amount never varies no matter the need); 2. learn French (always French, never Spanish or Czech as the need might demand); 3. learn gourmet cooking; and 4. polish all my silver. I even go so far as to buy the silver polish and tear up several perfectly good sheets for rags to do the actual work. But I never get any of these things done.

I do things like roam the aisles of Tuesday Morning Mall, buying everything they have on the "These are just a little bit hurt" rack—three gold Christmas tree balls in a box of four, a "Little Miss Cookie" coffee pot for an aspiring five-year-old cook who doesn't mind that there is no pot under the spout which dispenses the water, stuff like that. I spend a small fortune.

I don't need the bargain silver polish at Tuesday Morning since I have planned ahead and bought several bottles at full price weeks before he left, with the vow that the minute I can hear his car no longer I will polish each and every piece of silver I own, which will be quite a chore since I have not used any of it since 1960 when I got it for wedding presents. I will not polish it, of course, but I will take comfort from the fact that if I wanted to do so, I'd be prepared.

Do you get the picture?

Actually, when Louis' car hit the end of the driveway, I yelled, "Let the squalor begin!" and began blowing my nose on the sheets rather than getting up to get a handkerchief and eating vanilla Blue Bell ice cream with apricot preserves on top (my favorite breakfast treat next to Campbell's Tomato Bisque soup when he is gone) in bed with wild and happy abandon.

74

Do you still like me as much as you used to? Maybe like me but not respect me as much?

He'll be gone two weeks.

Expect a lot of mail!

Love,

Molly

"I don't ever want to be a bother . . ."

March 19, 1997

Billie,

I almost took Mattie to the eye doctor yesterday. She had called me at 7:30 A.M. to say that she was seeing double.

"I don't want to be any trouble to you," says she. "I KNOW how busy you are. If I bow my neck to the front about forty-five degrees, close my left eye and squint the right one almost shut, the double vision goes away. I'll just do that, so don't worry about me."

Right.

As you may recall, Louis is in Japan. He is always in Japan when his mother starts seeing double.

I hung up and called Kate to cover the shop for me. I threw on my clothes as I called the eye doctor and got an answering machine, of course. I told the machine to call me back the minute they opened at 8:00, giving the shop number.

Because I had just received an enormous shipment of Pendletons and the boxes were stacked all over the store, I jumped in the car and ran down there to push, pull, and unpack enough that Kate could make her way in and conduct business. The doctor's office called, and I assured the receptionist that this was an emergency. She gave us a work-us-in appointment and promised me that the wait would be a long one.

I left notes for the UPS man, and Crystal at the subshop, canceled a 10:00 book consultation, and a luncheon appointment, put gas in the car, remembered that I had left cats in the house and would need several bottles of Odor-O-No, and headed for Mattie's by 8:45.

She still had on her nightgown when I got there.

"Mattie," says I, "double vision is not something you mess around with. The doctor is expecting us. Throw your clothes on so we can get this show on the road!"

"Oh, I don't think we need to go after all," says she. "I just realized that the only time I have double vision is when I look out these front windows. They have storm windows on them so there are two panes of glass, one right on top of the other, and that can really distort your view, you know? I hope you haven't gone to any trouble for me. I don't ever want to be a bother."

And so it goes.

Love,
Molly

If dancing won't get the muse to unblock you, she'll try religion.

March 25, 1997

Sweet Billie,

I'm sure Dennis told you I called to see if you had made it home from the Poets and Writer's Conference in Tulsa Sunday, but he assured me you were a late riser and would no doubt be into Durant shortly. I should have remembered that you said you were going to sleep in and try to recoup your energy, but at my house, sleeping in means staying in the sack until 6:00 A.M. instead of 5:00 A.M., you will recall!

I am sorry to say, we can never become really good friends.

This is Tuesday, so Sister has no doubt been dancing on the lawn for you since early morning. Telling someone like her that you have a writer's block and need for her to help is a lot like calling 911. She will see to it that you become unlocked.

76

She told me on the tape this morning that she started dancing in the full moon Sunday night and continued through the eclipse. She became so exhausted that she finally passed out on the front porch, where the paper boy revived her about 5:45 A.M. But, knowing that you were in real trouble with your book, she jumped up, put her clothes back on, and started a round of church visits.

If dancing won't get the muse to unblock you, she'll try religion, she said. You do remember she is a church-of-the-month person, so she has lots of connections. But since this is Holy Week, some of the churches had other things to think about than your dinky book (their words, not mine!) so she didn't get as much cooperation as she might have, had this just been an ordinary week.

Did you ever think of scheduling your crises at a more convenient time for all of us? With Louis "Down Under" (That's AUSTRALIA, Billie, not what you are thinking! Stop reading all that pornography! In fact, get rid of your pornograph entirely. Everybody is switching to compact discs nowadays anyway!) . . . Anyway, with him gone I have been having to do awful things like fill the car with gas, water the lawn, put the garbage cans out on the curb. I have even had to COOK. I am going to be a whole lot nicer to him when he gets back, I think. I never knew there was so much to do until I had to do it! (That's a good line for somebody to say. I give it to you . . . free!)

Anyway, I know that by now you are so unblocked that you don't even have time to read my prattle. But I wanted to say that it was great fun being in your company last weekend, and once you get your book finished—check your calendar, which says that you WILL finish the book—we shall do lots and lots of fun weekends all over the world!

Sister told me that she is sending you a crystal which has magical powers. If you press it to your forehead, close your eyes, and chant, "I can write! I can write! I sure as hell can write," softly, you will become unblocked and finish *The Honk and Holler, Opening Soon* on deadline.

Try it. You'll like it. And it will no doubt leave an interesting indention on your forehead.

Love,
Molly

"I wish I had known I was happy."

May 1, 1997

Dear Billie,

Once in a while somebody jerks you up, grabs you by the neck, and hollers, "Look here! Listen to me! Shape up!"

It happened to me today. And she didn't even know she'd done it.

Early this morning, I was at the pharmacy picking up some nose drops because my nose was dripping and my head kind of hurt and I was all out of corn pads. A few minutes earlier I had found three wrinkles in my upper back, the only place left on my body that had no wrinkles. Until today. I noticed them in the full-length mirror some idiot installed in my bathroom. Mirrors should only be in the bathrooms of people you really hate.

Anyway, I was trudging down the aisle with a basket propping me up when I spotted Rita. Rita was a checker at our neighborhood Safeway when my kids were growing up years ago. It's been replaced by a Hastings, and there is not even a trace of the parking lot where Ginger took her first steps when I lifted her out of the grocery cart one cold February day. Rita was looking out the window when that happened, and she applauded. Rita was a redhead and so was Ginger. They bonded.

I had not seen Rita in ten or fifteen years. Her kids were about the same ages as mine, and you know how it goes in that kind of friendship. For years we had traded stories of broken arms, husbands who forgot stuff, teachers who were unfair. All the ticky-tacky of life. We greeted each other like long-lost sisters.

"Honey, how in the world are you?" I asked her, looking more closely at the deep, dark circles under her once-bright blue eyes and her unkempt red hair. That hair had been her glory.

"Oh, OK, I guess," she started and then thought better of it. "No, that's not the truth. The truth is I'm pretty awful. My husband is going blind. His mother is living with us. You remember she never liked me, but she ended up with us. Both kids are divorced and my grandkids are in all kinds of trouble."

78

"Oh, Rita, I'm so sorry," I said, giving her a squeeze. "I'm so sorry."

"You know," she went on, "when you and I knew each other, everything was out in front of us. Every day at the store there was something crazy and funny going on. I was so happy back then." She let a really long pause hang between us, gave a big sigh and said, "I wish I had known I was happy."

I wish I had known I was happy.
Those are words to live by, my dear. Words to live by.

Love,
Molly

"Follow the yellow brick road!"

May 13, 1997

Dear Billie,

As you have no doubt noticed, each of us is put on this earth with certain jobs to perform. You write, I sell, Sister gives happiness lessons.

Hers is not an easy task.

Most of her students do not like her. They do not want to be happy and they cannot imagine that she really is as happy as she seems to be. But she is. Most of the time she really, really is that happy. I have often asked her how she got that way and she replies simply, "I decide to be happy so I am."

And she does and she is.

Just this morning she gave me a lesson that made me laugh so hard that I would have wet my pants if I had had any on. I don't like to wear panties. They cut off my circulation. Anyway, I am walking down the street listening to Sister on the tape recorder as she babbles on about the wonderful strawberry bread she is going to bake when she gets home. This is in response to my telling her about winning a blue ribbon for MY pumpkin bread at the county fair in 1947 (I haven't done much cooking since then). She can't stand for me to be better than she, so she claims she has this fabulous secret recipe for strawberry bread which is going to be much better than my prize-winning pumpkin bread when she gets around to baking it. Just then she passed a house under construction. There were young men all over the roof hammering, nailing, and bantering with each other.

Shifting from her Betty Crocker persona to her happiness-lessons teacher, she cheerily called out, "Good morning! Isn't this a beautiful day?" (I could hear her on the tape.) I heard one of them reply, "This is the day the Lord hath made . . ."

And Sister finished, "Let us rejoice and be glad in it!"

The entire crew shouted, "Amen!"

I was so thankful that they hit her on a Christian Day. Think of how puzzled they would have been had their foreman shouted, "This is the day the Lord hath made . . ." and Sister shouted back, "Follow the yellow brick road!" because it was her Ozmund Day. Surely you remember her theory about the Wizard really being God? If not, be sure to ask her about it sometime, but only on a day when she is wearing those silly green glasses.

The Lord does, indeed, work in mysterious ways. And the day he made her was a glorious day for us all!

Love,
Molly

I don't think I'll ever cry
at a cemetery again.

May 24, 1997

Dear Billie,

I am so, so, so, so sorry that I have made up so many wild

tales in the past because I know that fact dulls my credibility. But bring on the Bibles because the following really happened.

This is Memorial Day weekend, and this is the day we make the journey to Anadarko to put flowers on my father-in-law's grave. It is not a day I enjoy as I am always the only one in my family who cries, and we all know that misery enjoys company.

Every year I swear I will not cry. I save up jokes to tell myself while we stand graveside. I write obscene words and put them on pieces of paper inside my shoes so I can slip the shoes off, see the words, and be so horrified that I am desecrating a sacred place with profanity that my eye sockets will be struck dry. In my mind I recite dirty limericks and hope for the same result.

Nothing works.

Until today.

As we approach the entrance to the cemetery, Mattie spies an old, dilapidated yellow oldsmobile, its trunk open, front door ajar, and a man kneeling at the nearby grave. "Oh, look!" she cries. "There's Chester! Let's go say 'Hello!'"

Mattie's relationship with Chester is best understood by the following little tale. When she moved here five years ago, she and I emptied forty-nine years of memories and junk into the dumpster with things like old lawn chairs with the webbing all broken out and boxes full of forty years of *Better Homes and Gardens* magazines. Then Chester would take over and spend the entire night emptying ALL of it into a wheel barrow and taking it to his house. After a couple of days of this, I asked Mattie the obvious, "Why don't we just give all this to Chester straight out and avoid the middle dumpster?"

To which she replied, "Oh, no. I don't really want Chester to have my things."

"But he's taking it anyway, Mattie."

"Yes, but that's not my fault," says she.

Back to the present, where Mattie has just cried out in a happy voice, "Oh, there's Chester! Let's go say 'Hello!'" and we are turning in to oblige her. Louis' jaw is set rather tightly I can see, but she's his mother and she has made a request.

The roads in this cemetery are so narrow that driving is really difficult, and our big car will not make the sharp turns.

By the time he is approaching the back of Chester's car, Chester is behind the wheel and driving off, the trunk still open. It seems to me that he did not spend an overly long period of time mourning whoever it was, but I don't say anything.

Louis follows rather slowly as the roads are quite bumpy. Chester turns up a new path, stops his car, gets out, picks up a wreath from a grave, puts it in the trunk of his car, jumps back in, and takes off.

I am the only one who is smiling. "He sure is driving fast," I venture. "Everybody else seems to be going real slow."

"Oh, Chester always did drive kind of wild," Mattie says.

Louis is concentrating on the narrow roads and stopping to let people go by. Chester's pattern is quite erratic.

"His family seems to be quite scattered," I say.

"Oh, Chester has always been good to take care of lots of people out here," Mattie replies.

I swear it is ten minutes and seven or eight graves before the light dawns in Louis' bulb. "Mother!" he exclaims. "He isn't putting flowers on anything. He's taking flowers off!"

"Oh," says Mattie with a benevolent sigh, "that's just Chester's way."

By this time I am literally laughing so hard I should be crying, but no tears will come because this is positively one of the funniest experiences I have ever enjoyed.

Louis takes the next turn which will lead to his father's grave, abandoning the chase entirely.

"Oh, well," sighs Mattie.

I'm watching Chester in the rear view mirror. He is now redistributing the wreaths on the graves of his near and dear.

Then he spots our car at Pop's grave.

"Here comes Chester," I say to Louis. "All that chasing and now he's coming to us."

Louis strides away at a fast military gate in order to avoid any contact whatsoever.

I wait to see what Mattie says to Chester.

"Why, Chester," she says, "we've been following you all over the cemetery for the last fifteen minutes!"

"Oh," replies Chester with a pious grin, "I have lots of folks that need takin' care of."

"And you're just the man to do it," says Mattie, patting him on the shoulder. "How have you been?"

I don't think I'll ever cry at a cemetery again.

Molly

The wooliest 10th Anniversary Party ever "herd" of

June 15, 1997

Dear Billie,

Even though half the year is almost gone, I am still surprised when I look at a calendar and see that it is 1997. I am equally amazed that my little bookshop/blanket place will be ten years old next month. I think I've told you that Daddy was a sign painter as well as a storekeeper and believed strongly in having professional-looking signs on a business and in the store itself.

"A tacky sign means tacky merchandise!" he always said. So I put the first big money I spent, $50, on a hand-painted "Levite of Apache" sign done by a wonderful old man named Eddie Greer who lives in Lawton. Mr. Greer was in his late seventies then, so his sign script looked like my dad's.

As I hung that first sign, which faced the west sun each day, I remember wondering if I'd stay in business long enough to have to have the sign repainted.

I've had to have it moved four times and repainted twice! The enclosed press releases tell the fun we have planned for our tenth anniversary gala. If the *Honk and Holler* is out by next summer, we'll feature you instead of a real live buffalo. How do you feel about that?

Love,
Molly

NEWS RELEASE

The buffalo will be roaming in Norman today at Levite of Apache, 113 Hal Muldrow Dr. Store owner and author Molly Levite Griffis will host Buffy the buffalo from 2-4 P.M. in celebration of the store's 10th anniversary.

The party theme comes from the book *The Buffalo in the Mall*, written by Griffis and illustrated by Kim Doner. Special guest at the event is, of course, Buffy.

Buffy is a four-year-old, 900-pound buffalo owned by Sheryl Robertson. She was bottle-fed and raised as a house pet. She still comes into the house for visits, but Buffy now roams a pasture near Beggs. She became a mother recently, much to Robertson's surprise, of a calf who is half buffalo, half zebu.

The buffalo will be outside of the store with her baby, "zebuffalo"—"unless we can get her through the door," said Griffis. Buffy likes to eat Gummy Bears, and will delight children of all ages as she eats out of their hands, she said.

Also on hand for the celebration will be folk singer Teresa Black. She has recorded an album titled "The Oklahoma Waltz." She will be performing the old Roger Miller favorite, "You Can't Roller Skate in a Buffalo Herd," and "Give me a home where the buffalo roam . . ."

A fourth generation Oklahoman, Black grew up in a large family. She heard firsthand tales of Oklahoma Territory in the 1800s. Her ballads and stories are taken from these family accounts.

Another local taking part in the celebration will be Norman illustrator Mike Wimmer. His artwork is featured in *All the Places to Love, Train Song, Bully for You, Teddy Roosevelt*, and *Flight: The Journey of Charles Lindbergh*.

Wimmer will be signing copies of his work along with Doner and Griffis.

In addition to working on *The Buffalo in the Mall*, Doner has also illustrated *Green Snake Ceremony*, winner of the Oklahoma Book Award, and *White Bead Ceremony*.

The Buffalo in the Mall is Griffis' first work. The book explains that among a myriad of possibilities, buffalo make the very best pets. To emphasize this point, Doner had Buffy the buffalo spend a few hours in her Tulsa home.

Buffy snacked out of the refrigerator, allowed her hair to be set in pink curlers and wandered from room to room as Doner took pictures. She wandered into the bathroom, but did not need to use the facilities.

"This promises to be the wooliest 10th Anniversary Party ever 'herd' of," Griffis said.

84

NEWS RELEASE
Buffalo to visit bookstore

A buffalo and her baby will make an appearance Sunday at the 10th Anniversary celebration of Levite of Apache bookstore.

The celebration will be held from 2 P.M. to 4 P.M. at The Levite of Apache bookstore at 113 Hal Muldrow Drive.

"Buffy" and her baby "Gemini" will be in front of the store for people to pet and feed, said store owner, Molly Griffis.

Book illustrator Kim Doner said she first heard of Buffy when she volunteered at an art museum during Native American Day.

"One of the things going on was a pet the buffalo area," Doner said.

Although buffaloes are known for their hot tempers, Doner said Buffy was docile while she was petting her.

"This big buffalo tongue comes out and sucks the gummy bears right out of my hand," she said.

Buffy is part of a menagerie of animals owned by professional truck driver Sheryl Robertson, Doner said.

Robertson recently brought the buffalo to Doner's house where she wandered from room to room.

"Now I have a home where the buffalo roam," Doner said.

Griffis and Doner will be autographing their book, *The Buffalo in the Mall.*

Griffis said she first got the idea for her book from a woman shopping for her granddaughter.

The woman's granddaughter wanted a pet, but was allergic to fur.

She bought a stuffed buffalo for her granddaughter and from this Griffis got the idea.

"If you're going to get a pet, get a buffalo," she said.

Local artist Mike Wimmer will also be signing books and art prints as part of the celebration, Griffis said.

Songs with a buffalo theme will be performed to celebrate Buffy's arrival, she said.

There will also be gummy bears, vanilla wafers and graham crackers on hand to feed Buffy, Griffis said.

Griffis said she wants to tie Buffy's visit with Oklahoma's 90th birthday Nov. 16.

A buffalo is the state animal, she said. Griffis said she wishes to encourage the public to celebrate Oklahoma's birthday.

"I should have belonged to Future Homemakers," he muses.

June 28, 1997

Dear Billie,

I hope you remember the letter I wrote you about my being a member of Future Homemakers of America in Apache. [See page 70.] If not, flip through your "Letts' Letters" and find and reread the FHA letter. You need a reference.

In that letter, I was elected district vice-president of the Future Homemakers of America because I took off my clothes and stood on my head while wearing a two-piece costume with "Molly for VP" emblazoned on the top half. I was a leader of young women.

Now, back to the future . . . Homemakers of America, that is.

This morning Louis was polishing the kitchen counter just after running the sweeper as I read the morning paper and drank my second cup of coffee.

"Listen to this," says I while munching on my toast. "Eleven members of the Duke, Oklahoma, chapter of the Future Homemakers of America won gold medals at the State Convention last week. They get to go to nationals. Imagine that, eleven of them from a little tiny town like Duke."

"Ummm," says Louis, who is checking his polishing job and looking around for what to clean next. Louis' goal in life is to wipe out squalor. That's his word for what I call untidyness—squalor.

"Hey," I go on, "get this. Some guy named Darran Scott won in the entrepreneurship division for developing a small-business plan. Darren Scott . . . a guy! And he belongs to the Future Homemakers of America in Duke!"

Louis is picking up dishes I left scattered around the living room last night. He marches to the dishwasher with them.

"I should have belonged to Future Homemakers of America," he muses. "Maybe I would have learned how to train you not to leave your dishes all over the place."

I don't think so.

Love,
Molly

Let him eat cake!

July 7, 1997

Dear Billie,

This is a wonderful world.

If you sometimes doubt that this is true, think on this story.

Yesterday morning I was juggling several boxes while attempting to enter the UPS office. I was about to have to twist my body at odd angles to get the door open with my free hand, so I prevailed on the young woman who was leaving at that time to hold the door for me.

"I about wrenched my back out the last time I tried this by myself," I chattered. "Doors can do you in!"

"That . . . and being married," she replied dryly as she reached for the hands of her three little kids under five who were watching all this with big eyes. They were all barefoot.

Her remark literally doubled over a neat black woman who was entering behind me. "Lord! Ain't it the truth!" she laughed. I told her to go first as I had forms to fill out.

"It's time for another batch to San Francisco next day air," she says to the girl behind the counter. "What time do I need to get it here to be sure it goes out right away?"

"Everything still leaves at 4:00 P.M.," says the UPS lady, who obviously knows this woman. "Bring it at five 'til 4:00."

"And you guarantee it will get to San Francisco the next day?"

"Guaranteed!"

"You promise? Cross your heart?"

"Cross my heart," says the UPS lady with a smile.

"How much is it going to cost me?" says Sadie. I named her Sadie in my head because I like the name Sadie and I like her.

"Forty dollars, just like last time."

Nothing has been weighed. No package is in sight.

I can't stand it.

"What are you sending to San Francisco?" I ask Sadie. And "How do you know how much it will cost without seeing the package or weighing it?" I ask Ms. UPS.

"Catfish," says Sadie.

"She does this all the time," adds Ms. UPS.

"Catfish?" I respond, with eyes as big as those kids of the poor woman who left and is missing all this fun. "You are next-day-airing catfish to San Francisco? San Francisco ... home of Fisherman's Wharf?"

"I caught 'em myself yesterday. Creek right south of here. My son says there's nothin' as good as his Mama's just-caught catfish."

"But ... but ... $40?" I question.

"That's not near as bad as what the barbecue cost me," she says with a shake of her head. "That stuff cost me $80. He says that nobody in the world makes barbecue like his Mama."

Is this not wonderful? I thought I made up good stories, but this is better than anything that I ever imagined.

"I think that is one lucky kid," says I, "to have such a Mama."

Sadie smiles.

And I try frantically to remember if I baked even one batch of cookies when George came home for Christmas from the Czech Republic last year.

How much do you think it would cost to next-day-air some slice and bake cookies to Prague?

That much?

Let him eat cake!

Love,
Betty Crocker, I'm Not!

Too busy looking for lost socks.

August 6, 1997

Dear Billie,

I just had an idea which will bring peace to the world in our lifetime even if that female white buffalo born in

88

Minnesota some time ago turns brown. You may remember that the Indians said that if she stayed white, peace would come to the earth.

We need it.

Peace, that is.

If not for the whole earth, at least at 812 Bob White where Louis discovered seven mateless socks which I had carefully secreted in an empty videotape box at the back of the storage case. He knows all my other hiding places, and I truly thought this space was safe. But no.

He was looking for his personal video of *The Maltese Falcon*, which he watches at least five times a year so he can gloat when Bogie lets the police haul the Mary Astor character off to jail.

"No broad's gonna get Bogie to lose his virtue," Louis growls as he watches the closeup of Bogie's face when his love is led away. But before he finds his video, Louis finds the unmatched socks and he growls at me instead. In a great imitation of Bogart, he demands that I produce the mates for those seven socks. He will not accept the fact that the washing machine ate them and threatens to get the San Francisco police involved since part of his brain is still fixed on the Falcon. Why, I ask you, why can't I just throw the damned things away as they appear? Because they are his socks, that's why. I routinely throw mine away without a second thought.

To solve this recurring problem, I propose the following chain letter:

Dear every woman who has to wash a man's socks,

This is a women-only MEN'S SOCK CLUB (WOMSOC for short). When you finish reading this letter, march to your hidy holes and dig out all those single, no-mate socks you have hidden. Stuff them into a manila envelope (or your husband's old army duffel bag) and mail them to the name at the top of the list.

Wait for your name to reach the top of the list. When it does, stuff all those unmatched socks in a used garbage sack and hide it at the bottom of the trash barrel. You've never seen any of those socks before. You are not even vaguely acquainted with the toes which have poked those holes. And there is not a man alive who would expect you to find mates to socks that were not his.

And the post office, which needs all the help it can get, will be subsidized by so much activity that a rate increase will no longer be necessary.

Peace in our time. It's up to you. Act now.

What do you think? If we could get either Oprah Winfrey or Rosie O'Donnell to endorse the idea, we'd be home free. Oh, wait! I just remembered. Neither of them is married. This is a problem only married women have. We could try Martha Stewart. No, wait, she's single too. In fact, I can't think of one successful woman in the world who is married. Is that because we are all too busy looking for lost socks?

Love,
Molly

Two miles and ten blisters later . . .

September 1, 1997

Dear Billie,

I loved the story you told last night about getting back into your dorm room by having someone lower the fire escape ladder. Why didn't I think of that? Here's my late-to-the-dorm story, which does not have as happy an ending as yours.

It was sometime in September of 1956, and I was a freshman at OU. Because you could have put the entire business district of my little hometown of Apache in the area called

Campus Corner, I thought—I really thought—that Campus Corner was downtown Norman. Actually, downtown Norman was a couple of miles north of my dorm and at least ten times bigger, but I hadn't figured that out. Yet.

I had noticed that there was a Boomer Theatre on Campus Corner, which was fairly near to my dorm. Therefore, when my very first college date said we'd be going to a picture show, I assumed we would go to the Boomer. I didn't know there was a Sooner Theater also (Boomer, Sooner, remember?) and that it was located in downtown Norman.

The date was at night, and I was so excited to be a college coed going out with a college man that I did not notice that the theater we drove up to was not on the Corner. After all, we had driven around for a while, and I was not familiar with Norman streets. I didn't have a car (no girl did) or much sense either. Nor did I notice that this was not the Boomer Theater but the Sooner Theater. Boomer, Sooner, Sooner, Boomer, they were both in the song, weren't they?

What with all the driving around, we were almost late and therefore had a hard time finding a parking place. My date, who was about as observant as I was, pulled in and parked in a tow-away zone. He bought our tickets, and we went in.

When we came out, the car was nowhere to be found.

"Oh," say I, trying to be cheerful, "it's not that far to Forbes House! We can walk!" I had on those wonderful two-and-a-half-inch high heels we all wore back then, remember?

"Are you sure?" says he, who knows that it is a couple of miles to my dorm, but does not have the money for cab fare.

"Of course, I'm sure, you lead the way!"

Two miles and ten blisters later, we trudge our way up to Forbes House where, not being as resourceful as you, I banged on the door to arouse the counselor who informed me that I was campused for the next month! No amount of pleading on my part softened her heart.

I wish I had known you and your fire-escape trick.

Thanks for buying our supper!

Molly

"You have salsa on the corner of your mouth . . ."

October 29, 1997

Dear Billie,

The world is divided into two very distinct groups. These groups have nothing to do with race, religion, or sexual orientation. On one side you have those who do not care if you have something on the corner of your mouth when you are eating. On the other side, you have those who passionately care that you have something on the corner of your mouth when you are eating.

It's as simple as that.

Louis, of course, is in the second group. I am in the first.

Last night when he came in, I rushed from the kitchen to the front door, all ready to tell him the most amazing, fascinating, unbelievable story I had ever told him. (I forget what it was about, but I know it was very important.) I had just scooped a big bite of salsa up with a chip, stuffed it into my mouth, chewed it a couple of times, and was in the process of swallowing it and starting my story at the same time, no mean feat.

"You are never going to believe this . . ." and I was just ready to launch into "Four totally naked men walked into the shop carrying dead oxen on their backs . . ." or some equally interesting tale, when he INTERRUPTED ME to say,

"You have salsa on the corner of your mouth."

Can you believe some people?

Do you think he has been married to me too long?

I have figured out why Daylight Savings Time makes me crazy. When you are getting dressed in the bedroom at 7:00 A.M. and you walk into the bathroom, a short walk of four or five feet, and by the time you get in the bathroom it is 8:00 A.M., you go crazy. I have never been able to reset all the clocks in the house in less than a week's period of time. So I run from room to room every time I need to pick up an hour or so because I have taken so long to read the paper. It just wears me out.

Are you home from Missouri? Did they wear you off? That's what Ginger always said as a little girl, "I'm all weared off."

As I sat by myself on the floor of my little shop signing Kim's 100 copies of *Buffalo in the Mall*, which had to be done in one sitting, I said to myself, "I thought being famous was going to be more glamorous than this!" From fifty on I was spelling my name "Moly Grifis" to cut down on the wear and tear on my hand.

Will we have to discount those?

Love,
Molly

December 1, 1997

This L.A. is really something! Saw a man wearing a skirt and in-line skates, a girl begging money so she could go to a movie, a guy kissing a guy and a dog wearing pearls and bicycle pants. This is the place for me!

We had dinner with Robbie Coltrane ("Cracker," a British police show) and went to a party where we met cinematographer of The Full Monty and Alfred Hitchcock's former assistant. Ain't we doing fine?!

Woke up to cloudy sky, mist, 73°. Read in the paper that you suffered 107°. I'm here—you're there. Why?

Dennis turns 64 tomorrow. (Not degrees, but years.)

Love you,
Betina Butz
(Billie)

I'd feel sorry for anybody who was sick, so don't feel special.

December 3, 1997

Dear Billie,

The Story of Molly's Illness
by Mattie L. Griffis, her mother-in-law

Molly has been sick with a cold for six days, thirteen hours, and twenty-seven minutes.

She caught the cold because she does too much and goes too fast.

And she never takes the vitamins I recommend:

500 units of C every day, double the dosage if starting to sniffle. (Molly has, by the way, sniffled a great deal these last six days, thirteen hours, and twenty-eight minutes.)

1,000 units of E daily.

50 units of zinc daily in months with an R in them. (Molly complains that zinc leaves a metal taste in her mouth for days, but I say better a metal taste in the mouth than mucus in the nostrils. That's what I think, anyway. Besides, Molly complains a lot. Especially for the last six days, thirteen hours and twenty-nine minutes).

In spite of my admonitions that she stay in bed, she has prolonged her illness by continuing to go to the shop. At my request, she stops by my house each day to pick up the things I have driven all over town to purchase for her and refuse to let her pay me for. The first day she was ill, I called to check on her and she said to me, "Mattie, you are so kind to be concerned about me."

To which I replied, "Well, I'd feel sorry for ANYBODY who was sick, so don't feel special."

She understood exactly what I meant.

When I visited her on Sunday, she said, "Now, I won't hug you like I usually do because I wouldn't want you to catch this."

And I said, "Oh, I won't catch what you have. I don't run myself into the ground doing too much like you do, and I always take my vitamins like you don't."

I have been driving all over town to buy her the kind of food she needs ... "feed a cold, starve a fever," I always say, but she claims that she is not hungry. I wouldn't want her to know it, but I think she enjoys all the attention she has had the past six days, thirteen hours, and thirty-two minutes.

But who's counting?

OK, I'll confess. I wrote this. But if Mattie could have, she would have!

I do love her!

And you!

Molly

"We got old . . ."

December 10, 1997

Dear Billie,

This is Wednesday.

As you know from previous Wednesdays, this is the day I take Marilyn to lunch.

Marilyn is my friend of thirty years who has Alzheimer's. She has been descending into her own private pit for five years now. Most sentences begin with, "and then I wanted ..." and end with "Texaco" as she reads the sign on the service station we are passing at that moment.

I almost bleed from the pores for this former computer wiz, this math major in college, this brightest woman I ever knew who now wears a watch which doesn't run—upside down. We both slid past sixty last summer. I knew when that happened. She didn't.

"What do you want to eat?" I chirp as always, praying

that this time—just this once—she'll say "Mexican!" But she knits her brows, looks horribly lost, and says, "It might and it might not . . ."

"Let's go where we always go," I say, turning the car in the direction it has gone for five long years and 256 Wednesdays. "We'll have chicken salad sandwiches!"

Her favorite.

But when we get there, things have changed. We have gone to the same place, to the same table for years now because change . . . noise . . . many things bother this once wonderfully bright, now sadly blank friend of mine. The place changed ownership last month, and I dreaded the change for her. And me.

The new owners, in an attempt to brighten up the place, have a Christmas tree with full regalia. On our table. The two-people table we have occupied for five years.

Marilyn is confused. I am temporarily desperate.

"There's a nice place we can sit," I say, steering her to the only other two-people table in the place. I do not have time to notice that it is next to a mirror. A very long, very clean mirror added in an attempt to make our little hole-in-the-wall look larger.

I take off her mittens, her coat, and her hat, get her seated and go to order the usual from a young woman who does not know us yet. A young woman who is learning.

"My friend has Alzheimer's," I explain as I have explained so many times before so strangers will judge our actions kindly. They always do. But I am also hoping this young girl will put a double slathering of mayonnaise on Marilyn's sandwich as did the previous owner. "She loves mayonnaise." I smile hopefully.

I sit back down and begin my weekly quiz which is always failed. "Do you know what day of the week this is?" It is always Wednesday, but, God love her, she never remembers.

"It's Wednesday," I prompt. "And what does that make tomorrow?"

"I might and I might not," is her reply.

"How about the month? This is December! It's almost Christmas! Remember Christmas?" I pray for a mention of Santa.

"Join the Army Reserve," she replies, reading the sign she reads almost every week. Signs are her specialty.

"I don't think I'll do that today," I laugh in an attempt to generate a reaction of some kind, any kind from her. "Maybe next week!"

As always, I keep trying to get her to connect and wondering at the same time why I torment her. "What is your husband's name?"

"You are trying to trick me," she says with a wan smile. And I fall silent.

It is at this time that she notices herself in the mirror to her left. She is first surprised, then intrigued. She studies her face intently.

"That's me," she finally concludes.

"That's right!" I reply, encouraged.

She looks more carefully and to her right where I am reflected. I peer at myself.

"And that's you," she says, mildly surprised.

"It sure is," I say. "You." I point. "And me." I point again.

She studies us both, tracing our faces and our gray hair carefully with her finger. There is a long pause.

"We got old," she says simply without a trace of regret or remorse.

"You're right," I say, turning my attention to our sandwiches which have just been served. "We have, indeed." And I bury my face in my napkin, pretending to blow my nose and trying very hard to not let her see me cry. Strangely enough, tears are one thing she seems to understand, and I don't want her to understand any of this.

Love,
Molly

"A little to the left, Thor."

January 5, 1998

Dear Billie,

My health club is killing me.

Have I remembered to tell you that I have joined a health club? One week ago, in a moment of temporary insanity, I plunked down $78, signed a form promising I would never sue if I injured myself, bought myself one of those yuppie water jugs to attach to my belt, and walked in with my eyes wide open. My eyes are the only part of my body that have not been sore since that day.

Actually, I stopped wearing my glasses to workout after the first day in a vain attempt to blur reality. I have never seen so much black, blonde and red hair in my life. Did you know there is a whole world out there that is under thirty and every one of them belongs to my health club?

I stood there the first morning in my baggy faded red pants, a t-shirt which reads "I Am Woman Hear Me Roar" given to me for Mother's Day some twenty-five years ago by my toddler children's not so funny father, and my Keds from Target.

In front of me were thirty some odd twenty-something females who had just opened boxes from Victoria's Secret Exercise Catalogue where they had maxed out their respective credit cards. Their socks matched their head bands. They had on makeup and perfume.

I don't know how they do it, but not one of those women sweats. Ever. No matter how many leg lifts, pec rolls, ab busts, they never never sweat. And they try to avoid having eye contact with me.

There is one plus in all of this, however. His name is Thor. It says so right on his shirt.

Thor is twenty-nine.

Thor works out a whole lot and has developed all parts of his body both seen and unseen. Even with my glasses off I can see some things quite clearly.

Thor is my personal trainer.

That is somebody who trains you. Personally.

He shows me how to use the equipment and strokes my pecks and abs and stuff like that to see if I am doing things right.

I am often a slow learner, and he has to do it again and again.

I stave myself from saying, "A little to the left, Thor."

Do you think this is going to make me live longer?

Oh, I hope so.

Love,
Molly

"The wind can't blow these cards away!"

January 15, 1998

Dear Billie,

Because I know that you write on a wonderful old fashioned typewriter, I hate to bring up the "C" word, but I must.

Computer.

There, I've said it!

"Fingers that touch keys will never be these," I always say.

My sister and brother-in-law brought an orphan computer into their home some years ago. It was left on their doorstep by an unwed monitor (me) who had purchased the damn thing in the middle of a hot flash and thought better of it when my fever broke. I even went to the trouble of enrolling in a class at our local vo-tech school. After three one-hour sessions where the teacher babbled enthusiastically about bytes and bits, I cornered her after class and said, "I will not be here tomorrow night. If we ever see each other in public, you are not to acknowledge that we have ever met. I do not want my money back. You can give this $60 book to any poor, misguided soul who might wander into this room. Tomorrow night, when I am not here, and on the succeeding nights when I am not here, you are not to say, 'Does anybody know what has happened to Mrs. Griffis?' You will know that Mrs. Griffis has gone on with her life."

My brother-in-law, Jim, is the type who likes to have whatever is the "in" thing. But after getting the "in" thing, he usually wants "out." That computer I gave them was outdated before they learned how to turn it on. Anyhow, it was a used one to begin with, and they decided that it had come to them with certain genetic flaws they would have never overcome had they ever figured out how to turn it on. Besides that, they were both working and busy.

Then they retired and had lots of time on their hands and fingers. So they traded that first computer in on a brand new, state-of-the-OnLine $3,000 job that does everything but floss their teeth. In preparation for this purchase, both my sister and brother-in-law enrolled in four classes at the local vo-tech school to learn computerese. They took Beginning I; Beginning Again (for those with a failed first); Really Getting Serious; and Dos for Dummies.

They were ready.

Having bought from "Sam's–Great Bargains, No Service" they had to pay some guy $60 an hour to come and show them how to operate their wonderful machine that was going to build them a bridge to the 21st century. Our vice president told them so. The guy stayed two hours, pocketed his $120, took his hammer, nails, and other bridge-building materials, and left. It has been a week now that these two sixty-five-year-olds have lived in the Wonderful Wizard of Computland. And here are the results.

They now have two phone lines and therefore get twice as many calls wanting to clean their rugs, spray their lawns, and neuter their cats. They can't figure out how to unplug either line. Jim has played 105 games of Solitaire, which I hesitated to point out he could have done with a $1.50 deck of cards.

"How many games did you win?" I ask.

"That's not the point," says he. "The point is that the wind can't blow these cards away!"

"Did the $60-an-hour guy point that out or did you figure that out all by yourself?" I want to know.

Give me a lead pencil and crank sharpener any day.

Love,
Molly

. . . even napkins with strawberries on them, for God's sake.

Dear Billie,

Today is Super Bowl Sunday, and Martha Stewart's love child, to whom I am married, is doing it again. . . taking over my party. Every once in a while, I crave company, and he, who thinks a party of one is the best kind if he is the one, reluctantly goes along. Then, as time for my gala nears, he begins to take over.

Now, a "gala" at our house is when we ask one other couple over for hamburgers. I do make homemade hamburger buns and homemade potato salad. That's what makes it a "gala." It also is how I get Louis to agree to have guests. As I have told you before, he is strange. But he makes me laugh. Most of the time.

Anyway, here I am preparing for company (actually I'm writing you a letter, aren't I?) and he is saying things like, "I think you should empty the waste baskets and make the bed before they come." I keep on typing. Then he decides to go to the store, and I know my plans for a gentle day are going down the tubes.

He comes home with fresh strawberries. "You needed dessert," says he. With a flourish he takes out the strawberries and that chocolate stuff you melt and dip the strawberries in. He also has purchased a matching plate (strawberries around the rim) to put the chocolate dipped strawberries on. He even

101

has napkins with strawberries on them, for God's sake. The man is insane. I am surprised that he has not flown to Los Angeles to Gumps for napkin rings to match the napkins. Napkin rings are very, very important to Louis. (Martha Stewart is his REAL mother, remember?) But he assures me that the green napkin rings, ones we already own, will look like leaves.

I sure hope he has arranged for the uniforms on whatever teams are in the Super Bowl to match our tablecloth.

Molly

We fit, he and I. We just fit.

February 25, 1998

Dear Billie,

As you no doubt read in the paper, I lost the "Number One Hoss" in my stable of writers yesterday. That's what I teasingly called Harold Keith, that wonderful old guy you met from time to time in the shop. He won the Newbery Medal for his *Rifles for Watie* in 1957, and I was lucky enough to get to publish and reprint his books when he got old and everybody forgot about him. Keep that in mind, dear heart. No matter how famous you become as a writer, if you outlive your contemporaries—agents, editors, and publishing house connections—you just might have to depend on a risk-taker such as I to keep your words alive.

Mr. Keith walked into my office and my life eight years ago and slipped out of both my life and the tattered old cover on his body on the evening of February 24, 1998. While he was ready to finish his last race (he was a track star in college and ran until he was ninety-two!), I was not quite prepared for that final starting gun to be fired.

I had met Mr. Keith in the sixties and seventies when I took books to his home for him to autograph for my kids. He was a good friend of our friend "Red" Reid, who had been the ticket manager at the University of Oklahoma during Mr. Keith's thirty-nine-year tenure as sports information director there.

When I was starting the third year of my publishing house, Red suggested that I approach Mr. Keith about reprinting some of the children's books for which he had become famous. All but one, the Newbery winner, were out of print.

"I'll soften him up for you," Red promised.

In retrospect, I realize that Mr. Keith needed more than a bit of "softening up" as his impressions of me as a publisher were that I was a girl, quite young, and had no idea what I was doing.

He was right on all counts. I was a female in the male-dominated world of publishing. I was fifty and he was eighty-five; young depends on the quarter you are playing in. I had published eight books winging my way along on chutzbah and the "blatant exhibitionism" I mentioned in a letter a few months ago.

Mr. Keith, who in his day and time was famous for knowing how to generate publicity for the University of Oklahoma football teams, certainly knew how to draw a crowd, how to generate lots of newspaper ink, but an exhibitionist he was not, blatant or otherwise.

It took him a while to get used to me.

When I visited him that last time in the hospital, I looked at that frail little ninety-four-year-old body huddled in that big, white bed, and I shivered for him.

"Mr. Keith, are you warm enough? I started to bring you a Pendleton. They are mighty warm," I assured him.

"You never quit, do you?" he grinned. "You think if I die and they take my picture and I'm wrapped in a Pendleton blanket, that might sell a few blankets, don't you?"

I laughed through tears that were starting.

We fit, he and I. We just fit.

And we had eight years together.

But to paraphrase the title of an old TV sitcom, eight was not enough.

In sorrow,
Molly

When Opal's ketchup hit Ethel's blouse, pandemonium broke loose.

March 11, 1998

Dear Billie,

I just realized that I have never introduced you to Aunt Opal and her sister Ethel, so I will do so today. Remembering them always makes me laugh. I hope the same will be said of me when I'm gone.

Opal and Ethel (their real names as there are no innocents in this family) were sisters, but not sisters like Sister and I are sisters. While they did share the same father and mother, Opal and Ethel were not overly fond of each other, to put it mildly, which they rarely did.

They were my kin in a round about sort of way. Their sister Mae was my father's first wife. She died in the flu epidemic of 1917. Then a year or so later, my father's brother Abe married Opal, making Opal my aunt.

Anyway, as they aged, I inherited both Opal and Ethel as neither had children, and Opal was my father's dead brother's wife, and Ethel was the sister of my father's dead wife. Death creates strange relationships.

They each lived alone, Opal in a house she had shared with Uncle Abe for fifty-seven years, and Ethel in a tiny, dreary apartment. It was rumored that Ethel smoked and had a drink from time to time, which Opal never did. They detested each other. I liked Ethel best, of course.

One sultry day in July when they were both in their eighties, Opal and Ethel called to say they had decided to move to apartments in Spanish Cove Retirement Village. This in spite of the fact that neither of them spoke a word of Spanish and rarely spoke to each other for that matter. They had already signed leases on the adjoining apartments by the time they called me. I was amazed.

"This way we can keep an eye on each other," Opal explained to me. I knew for a fact they had gone for months at a time, maybe even years, not speaking.

"You better not be looking in my windows!" I heard Ethel yell in the background.

"Could you help us with the moves, dear?" Opal asked sweetly. "We'd really appreciate it."

I took a deep breath and agreed to do so.

I could easily write an entire book on moving day, but for this letter, I'll confine myself to our moving day lunch at McDonald's. Until we walked in, it never occurred to me that there were citizens of the United States who had never been in a McDonald's or any other fast food restaurant for that matter. In fact, I began to realize after I got them there that Opal and Ethel had never really entered the 20th century. They were completely and utterly amazed.

"Look at that menu all lit up!" Opal cried.

"Look at that cup dropping down all by itself and soda pop running in there!" Ethel yelled back. They had packed their hearing aids in moving boxes.

Deciding what to order took a very long time.

The little styrofoam boxes the burgers came in simply blew them away. They had never seen such things in their lives, they kept telling anybody who would listen. It was wonderful.

But not as wonderful as the condiments table. They had never seen little tiny packages of salt. They had never seen little pepper packages. But most of all, they had never seen little tiny packages of mayonnaise, mustard, and ketchup. They wanted to know the prices of these wonderful little things. When I told them the condiments were free, they lost their minds and filled their purses. By this time, the entire place was watching us.

We got our orders and found an empty table. I was enjoying myself immensely and taking my first bite when Ethel ripped open her mustard package, shooting its contents onto the front of Opal's pale pink silk blouse. Her favorite one.

As fate would have it, Opal was opening her ketchup at the same moment with the same result, only Ethel's blouse was white. When Opal's ketchup hit Ethel's blouse, pandemonium broke loose.

I will leave it to your imagination to picture a food fight at McDonald's started by two slightly deaf eighty-year-old sisters who didn't care for each other to begin with and disliked each other even more by the end of the lunch hour.

As I said earlier, I could write a book.

Love,
Molly

Leon's name is just Leon.

April 29, 1998

Dear Sister B.,

When I sent you the letter I had received where the woman explained her unusual name, it reminded me that maybe I had not told you about my uncles.

Molly, my Polish-born grandmother, was so proud to be an American citizen she named six of her sons for presidents. Daddy was George Washington Levite; Uncle Abe, Abraham Lincoln Levite; Uncle Bill, William McKinley Levite, right on down the line until the seventh and final son whom she named . . . Leon.

Now, when I got old enough to learn about presidents of the United States and discovered this discrepancy, I asked Sister, who is six years older and therefore much wiser, why poor old Uncle Leon just got named Leon instead of a fancy presidential name. She lied through her teeth, as she often did when I asked her something important, and said, "Oh, Uncle Leon's REAL name is Ponce de Leon. They called him Leon for short." I told that story with pride for years before Mama heard me telling it one day and said, "What are you talking about? Leon's name is just Leon. Where did you get such a story?"

Guess that proves that some storytellers are made, not born, doesn't it? Sister was made. I was born.

Speaking of born, today is George's 31st birthday. It

makes me crazy that he is so far away that I can't bake him a cake. It takes packages so long to get from here to the Czech Republic that even chocolate chip cookies, his favorite, are either stale or completely crumbled by the time they arrive. I'm sure you know how I feel with Shawn half a world away also. They do grow up and take wings, don't they? And I truly wouldn't have it any other way.

And yet . . . and yet. I sure would like to see him more often.

Molly

. . . every record
Lawrence Welk ever made.

May 19, 1998

Dearest Billie,

Well, there is nothing left in the world for me to wish for so I might as well die, but not until I spend a few years dancing, singing, and twirling.

I acquired the last item on my list today. You know how when you are young you dream and make lists of all the things you'd like to acquire in your lifetime, things like white majorette boots (can still wear them and often do); a fire baton to go with the boots (had it for one day as I set fire to the front yard when I dropped it); a combination radio/alarm clock that could be set to go off AFTER you fall asleep (high school graduation present); a college degree (U. of Okla. 1960); a good husband (Louis Griffis, 1960); children (George, 1967, and Ginger, 1970); a 1950 Chevy (1972 and 1988, same car, bought it twice); a blond ceramic cocker spaniel dog (don't ask, just know that I got her, and her name is Honey); and finally (my wants were few and rather simple as you no doubt noticed), a jukebox. . . a real live genuine working Wurlitzer.

107

I got the jukebox today. Along with 250 records including—you won't believe my luck on this—every record Lawrence Welk ever made. Is that not "cool," as the young are wont to say . . . and say . . . and SAY when they are not saying "like"?

It was delivered to my shop at 2:37 P.M. Daylight Savings Time. By 2:47 I had worked up a real sweat. I punched buttons and danced. I punched buttons and sang. I punched buttons and twirled (no, not fire, just rubber-tipped) and I punched buttons and gloried in the fact that I am positively the luckiest, happiest, craziest human being I know. And I know a lot of people. Come onna my store, and I'll let you punch all the buttons you want.

For free.

Except for Lawrence Welk. I charge for his records in hopes that that will keep them from wearing out.

Musically yours,
M.G.

"Your Squaw Is on the Warpath"

May 20, 1998

Dear Billie,

I hate to tell you, but I think my jukebox is going to be the death of me yet. You know that I would have never plunked down that much hard-earned cash if it had not been for the party I am going to throw for you for *The Honk and Holler Opening Soon*. I had to have a jukebox or nobody would come, right? We won't mention the fact that I have lusted after a Wurlitzer for many a year or that I now do nothing but dance to its sweet music when I should be writing. I prefer to blame my troubles on the release of your new book, forcing me to buy a jukebox. And a restaurant booth. And a bubble machine.

Anyway, the very first day the juke arrived, it almost caused me to have a heart attack. I was dancing in front of it to "You Ain't Woman Enough to Take My Man" and reading all the delicious 50s titles... Elvis' "I Want You, I Need You"... Gale Storm's "Why Do Fools Fall in Love" ... when I got to B17, which was titled "Your Squaw Is On the Warpath."

How was it going to look to have "Your Squaw Is On the Warpath" playing in a Pendleton blanket shop that prides itself on its multicultural ambiance? I had never heard the words, of course, but the title alone made me think that this might be a record I would want to replace. I glanced around to be sure the shop was empty and pushed B17, thinking all the while how extra funny it would have been had this particular song been B7 and therefore Vena Takes Horse's favorite.* What was B7, by the way? It made me crazy that you never told!

Just as I punched, a car drove up and five Native Americans I did not know got out and headed for my door. Now I am certain that any and all of my regulars—red, white, or black—would have hooted at being greeted by "Your Squaw Is On the Warpath." But these were out-of-towners who didn't know that my grandfather was the first Pendleton dealer in the Twin Territories. Didn't know he had been picked by the Indians themselves because they knew he would deal fairly with them. They didn't know that "my family would have starved to death in the early days if it hadn't been for the Indians." (A direct quote from my Grandfather Pete.)

By the time they walked in, "You Ain't Woman Enough to Take My Man" was going to be over and "Your Squaw Is On the Warpath" would be their introduction to the Levite's Pendleton Shop. They might think it funny, but I fully understand how the white man's shabby treatment of them over the years might make them feel that the song was not at all appropriate.

I had no idea how to turn the darn thing off. Where was Vena Takes Horse when I needed her? In desperation, I dove for the jukebox's cord and jerked it out of the wall.

As it turns out, they were such neat people that I ended up telling them what almost happened, and we all laughed and

[*Vena Takes Horse is a character in The Honk and Holler, Opening Soon.]

listened to "Your Squaw Is On the Warpath" together. They thought it was funny, and I was relieved.

These days, my family would not "starve to death" without them, but my life would be much poorer if it weren't for the Indians. Not because they buy blankets, but because they laugh and cry with me and are my friends. And they hardly ever go on the warpath, even if provoked by irreverent songs.

In the band . . .
Molly

Can Sister and I throw a party or what?

June 12, 1998

Dearest author of the best selling book
in Norman, Oklahoma!

Well, this is the day after the night before, the night before being your autograph party for *The Honk and Holler, Opening Soon* at Levite of Apache, that Pendleton-blanket-selling bookstore in Norman, Oklahoma. I say that so you won't get it confused with other Pendleton-blanket-selling bookstores in other towns and states. After a while I am sure they all begin to look alike.

Well, there is no other word for it: You ruled. I know that old fogies such as I do not use "rule" in that context, but "rule" you did. Even if you did get lost and missed the radio station interview!

I felt so, so sorry for you when you staggered in after two hours of trying to find a way to turn around and come back on that turnpike to Lawton. There is no way! I was only frantic because I thought you had had a wreck. I routinely get lost driving home from my shop. We moved to a new house, remember? I have only lived in that new house three years. After twenty-nine years, my car goes to the old Trenton Road

110

address automatically, so I totally understand the meaning of the word "lost."

But back to the good stuff. Can Sister and I throw a party or what? What was the best part for you?

Was it the jukebox which continually played B-7, which everyone was amazed to find was Lawrence Welk's "Pennsylvania Polka?" Who would have guessed that that was Vena Takes Horse's favorite song? Not I! You do know that the only reason I paid $2,500 for that infernal machine was because you wrote a book that had a jukebox in it, and I had to have a jukebox for your autograph party! (Please destroy the letter where I said that I had wanted a Wurlitzer my entire life. It might make my credibility suspect.)

Or was it the carhops who delivered your books on metal trays which had been resurrected from Sister's attic? Did I remember to tell you that Daddy bought those when he bought out a drive-in sometime in the 50s? He was always buying out the stock of some place or another, so we have some wonderful stuff from the "olden days." They were just languishing in her attic waiting to serve books to the customers at *The Honk and Holler*.

My only regret is that our carhops could not be on roller skates in the parking lot like you used to wear when you were a roller-skating carhop. OSHA, that ever present watchdog of safety, declared that our parking lot was not "user friendly." In other words, my own Sister could have sued me for my half of our company if she fell and broke her leg. Or hip. Again. (I'll tell you the truth about her broken hip on another day.)

Or was the best part the little aprons the carhops wore which were emblazoned "Honk and Holler"? I thought those a very nice touch. Did I tell you that Warner Books paid for the aprons via their co-op program? They are a fine publishing house, as I am sure you know by now. That Tina is quite a lady! I don't know if you had enough time to notice because you were so busy signing and talking to those who loved Novalee, but those carhops were quite skilled at delivering Cokes when they weren't delivering books, although most of the time the place was so packed that they could barely make their way back to the Coke dispenser.

By the way, I borrowed Crystal of the Red Cowboy Boots'

ice scoops and in all the hubub they got lost. I live in fear that in retaliation for her loss she is going to tell Louis that I eat a BLT every month, sometimes twice a month. You know what a talker Crystal is. Please put her in your next book, perhaps as the heroine, so she will forgive me and keep her mouth shut. After all, it is really your fault that I lost her ice scoops.

Other than the lost ice scoops, it was a glorious night, wasn't it?

Your "weared off" friend,
Molly

June 15, 1998

Dear Molly,

Here, at last, the "formal" thank you for the best damned signing <u>any</u> author <u>ever</u> had. It was extraordinary, surprising, great fun and wonderful!

You have—since the day we met—been the most loyal and determined, of all the booksellers, to pull me through as I drag the <u>Heart</u> and the <u>Honk</u> behind me.

I will probably never make the NY Times Best Sellers List ... but it will <u>not</u> be because Molly Griffis didn't give it her <u>very best shot</u>.

Always—
Billie

"Give me Mr. Sheraton."

June 16, 1998

Dear Billie,

I know I am going to see you in DeSoto, Texas, tomorrow, but this was a story that simply could not wait. My mind may not be with me by then.

Joel, that wonderful Mennonite from Kansas who is at least eighty but looks forty (a real testimony to clean living), called this afternoon to say that he was FED-Xing the most stunning poster in the world to our hotel in Austin. It has seven color photos of the Levite of Apache Honk and Holler signing captioned with "LETT'S CELEBRATE!" He carefully spelled it for me, and then asked the inevitable question. "Lett's? Letts'?" When he found out your name was Letts instead of Lett, I had a lot of quick talking to do to convince him that ninety-nine former English students of yours and mine out of one hundred would never notice the misplacement of the apostrophe.

Because he was so proud and because I know what awful things can happen to anything left to chance, I telephoned the Austin Sheraton to inform them that they should be on the lookout for the posters being shipped in my name. I added rather parenthetically that I would also like to lengthen my stay as I would arrive in Austin on June 18. I already had a reservation for the 19th.

The desk clerk informed me that nobody by my name was registered at that Sheraton for any day, any time, ever.

I smiled to myself at his naivete and gave him my confirmation number, thinking how clever I was to have recorded it, along with the name of the clerk taking my reservation, Deborah. (I even knew Deborah's mother's birthday because it was the same as my Aunt Opal's and two days before Pearl Harbor. We had become rather close, Deborah and I. Her mother hates purple and says cucumbers "repeat" on her.)

Which made it all the more distressing when I heard him say, "Sorry, madam. That is an invalid confirmation number. No one is registered in the name of Griffis."

"Silly boy," says I, "of course I am registered. Look under Levite of Apache."

"What?" And I explain about the Bible and the Indian tribe, and prepositions.

He checked again.

"We have no such number. And I am sorry to say that the hotel is booked for that night. And for the night before. Booked solid."

"Now just a minute," says I. "I have a confirmation number. You took my credit card."

"Not I, madam," says he. "I only started working here today."

Ah-ha!

"Well, then give me someone with longevity." I explain what that means.

I am passed to John, who has worked there for at least a week. We go through the same song, second verse.

"There are two Sheratons in Austin," says he. "You obviously made your reservation at the other one."

"Do you have a reservation for Billie Letts? It should be flagged with a VIP sticker. I talked at length with Deborah Friday. Deborah is coming to the autograph party at Book People with her mother (Anna) and Deborah confirmed both my and Billie's reservations. I know I have the right place. Otherwise, how would I know Deborah's mother's name?"

"I'm sorry, but we have no reservation for Billie Lett," says Joel's cousin.

"That's *Letts*," I say, nearing the breaking point.

"Nope, neither one of you is here," says he.

"Give me Mr. Sheraton," I say in a no-nonsense tone. "Right now."

"What?"

"Young man, I promise you that I shall drive straight to your hotel, take off all my clothes and walk through the lobby with a sign that says, 'This is what Room Service here did to me,' emblazoned across my chest if you do not get me somebody in charge immediately."

114

"This is Keeley," says a female voice. "May I help you?"

"What is your last name, Keeley?" I inquire.

"We only go by first names here," says she.

"And why is that, Keeley?" I push. "What are you trying to hide?" I know I'm out of control, but I've been on this damn phone nigh on to 45 minutes by now.

Keeley takes all the information starting from the time my mother went into labor with me, and says she'll be back. Ten minutes later, she is indeed back with all the same "You have the wrong Sheraton, that is not a valid confirmation number, you have no reservation" tale.

"Talk to someone higher up, Keeley," I demand. "Now!"

And to my amazement, she does. She comes back twenty minutes later to say, "I am so sorry, Mrs. Griffis, we found both your number and reservation and Mrs. Letts' number and reservation. I have no idea how this all happened. You are all set. Have a nice evening."

So there you have it. I bet the Austin Sheraton would serve Deborah's mother cucumbers, don't you?

'Til then,
Molly

"I don't read much really."

June 22, 1998

Billie, my friend,

I want you to know that I am forfeiting a Fred Astaire–Eleanor Powell movie, *Holiday*, to write and send you the first Letts letter to be faxed in its original form. I had to call Jamie Raab to get your hotel in Missouri, but after our exhausting joint Texas escapade, I felt you needed all the endorphins you could get. This is going to be one healthy dose.

115

The phone rang early at the shop today.

Me: Levite of Apache.

Unknown Female Voice: Let me speak to Billie Letts.

Me: (In a bit of an amazed voice) Uh, she's not here. I had her for an autograph party on June 11, but she's traveled thousands of miles since then. I do have autographed copies of both of her books. How many would you like for me to save for you? Or I could mail them if you are out-of-town.

Unknown Female: Well! (Petulance of the first order) WE have been trying to get together for a year and a half! I have a manuscript that I want her to read! I can't believe that she was here in town and didn't let me know!

Me: (Pedaling my bike backwards as fast as I can) Oh, well, yes, I see, I see very clearly now. (I almost burst into song with those lyrics.) She looked for you all evening.

U.F.V.: She did?

Me: Absolutely. Now, how many copies of her new *The Honk and Holler, Opening Soon* did you want to order? I only have six left that are autographed, but I can order more and get her to sign them. I have eleven of *Where the Heart Is*. I've got my pencil ready.

U.F.V.: Then she's not there now?

Me: Well, no, not at the moment. But I can take your order without her being here. She doesn't mind, really. I'm sure she thinks of you often. Did you want all six of those inscribed to you? And would you mind spelling your name? Slowly.

U.F.V.: Oh, no. I don't want to order any of her books. I don't read much really. I just want her to read my book and give me some suggestions. It's the story of my life from birth to thirteen including detailed accounts of my five years with a manic depressive piano instructor who would never allow me to play in her presence.

Me: Well, I hate to interrupt, but I hear my other line beeping, and I'm going to have to hang up now. I am sure that Billie will be in touch with you soon.

U.F.V.: But I have moved since I wrote to her last.

Me: I'm sure she'll be able to find you. Warner Books is a very efficient publishing company, and they keep her abreast of all current events and addresses.

U.F.V.: But . . .

Me: Click . . .

I'll never reveal your whereabouts!

Molly

"Sell it!"

June 25, 1998

Billie,

Wanted you to see the letter I sent to Bob Peterson after you called to read me his column from *The Durant Daily Democrat* about my wild and wonderful (says she modestly) autograph party for you last week. As you saw in the article, Bob and I go way back as he lived in Norman when I was in school at OU. That old saying about a prophet being without honor in his (her, in your case!) own country doesn't ring true with people from Durant, America, does it? Even the home town folks love you, but now that I think of it, you aren't a prophet, are you? Don't become one or you'll lose your honor! Here's my letter to Bob!

June 26, 1998

Dear Bob,

I was delighted with your column which Billie read to me in its entirety over the phone five minutes after she read it and called you. What a nice thing for you to do and say!

Billie and I did a book signing tour of Texas last week and discovered that Texas is, indeed, a very large state! Between us we hit Dallas, De Soto, Longview, Austin, and Georgetown. She was signing her two, of course, and I was signing my *The Buffalo in the Mall*. Then I got to come home to my "own sit down" as the Indians in Apache used to call home, but poor Billie had to hit Denver and Kansas City before she got to go back to Durant. I decided never to become a rich and famous writer after watching her and seeing what was required!

I have been writing to Billie ever since she walked into my shop a few months after *Where the Heart Is* was released. She put a copy in my hand and said, "I understand you really know how to sell books. I wrote this one. Sell it!" And I did. And have. Hundreds and hundreds of them in my little bitty shop one block from Hastings, and less than a mile from the twin giants called Barnes and Noble and Borders. Norman has changed a great deal since you lived here.

Sister and I are going to do our best to get to Billie's signing at the bookstore there in Durant next week. If so, we'll look you up! You knew me when my body was much lighter and my hair much darker, I might add, so I'll be the one with a *Honk and Holler* apron on. That's what my carhops wore!

Best to Sarah!
Molly

The best laid plans
of lizards and cats . . .

July 2, 1998

Dear Billie,

I wanted so badly to call you on this one, but it is only 1:00 in the afternoon, and I know that you are not an early riser so I'll Letts Letter you.

I was so glad that I called on your birthday, even though I woke you up and you made no sense whatsoever. It's the thought that counts even though I had no idea it was your birthday. You are right; I am a clairvoyant and would be a better one if I could spell it without looking it up. The sixty roses smelled wonderful! What a neat husband you have!

Now, to today's story that I really, really wanted to tell you on the phone in person. Do you believe me any better when I tell you these stories than when I write them to you?

As we speak (actually as I write) Louis is on his way to Oklahoma City to pick up Mr. Nakamoto. He is one of the Japanese contingency which were so very good to Louis and Ginger while she was launching the ship in Japan back in March, remember? They will drive back to Norman, get me and then go to dinner (actually late lunch/early supper since it is twelve hours later in Japan, so who knows what meal it is for Kaz, which is what Ginger called him; he's about her age) at a wonderful German restaurant. Then Louis and I will drive him back to Oklahoma City, where he is staying.

Now to understand the elaborate cleaning preparations necessary for Mr. Nakamoto's visit, I need to invade Louis' privacy. You have no doubt seen *The Odd Couple*. Well, that is Louis and me. He's Oscar and I'm Felix, or is it that other way around? Being the disorganized one, I don't remember which was the neat freak, and which the slob. But in our *Odd Couple*, I'm the slob. Only yesterday, Louis had me cleaning the squalor from our garage floor with a very small red brush. I was doing this, he said, so that the new neighbors, who were just moving in, would

119

see me and understand the standards expected in our neighborhood. Louis hoped to convince them that I did this weekly.

The truth of that story is that one of our three cats refuses to use the litter box. Instead, he uses a hard, cold corner of concrete to "tend to nature" (Aunt Opal's term) and therefore creates quite a mess through the winter months. I give it a cursory cleaning daily, but when July comes, Louis says, "Enough is enough!" and I do my once-a-year scrub job.

Once a year.

Not once a week.

Latrine detail.

Not spit and polish.

I've never learned to use the oven in this house, remember? Who in their right mind would believe I scrub the garage floor weekly?

The new neighbors, that's who. The wife saw me and refused to move into a neighborhood where people scrubbed the floors of their garages. I admired their courage.

You begin to get the picture of what kind of cleaning that had been done in our house in preparation for Mr. Nakamoto.

It was clean. It was perfect. The health department would have given us a certificate.

That was because I had hired the "Merry Maids" at $75 an hour to see to it that a couple of years of squalor (Louis' favorite word) was eradicated. They left at midnight.

I was not allowed out of bed until nearly noon of THE BIG DAY. The crumbs from my midnight snack were covered by the sheet when Louis made the bed this morning.

No house has ever been so clean. Until fifteen minutes before Louis was to leave for his leisurely drive to Oklahoma City in which he planned to muse on his clean, clean *casa*.

Fifteen minutes before he was to leave for the 1:00 pickup of Mr. Nakamoto, Ming the Magnificent, our middle cat, named for a character in Flash Gordon, scratched at the front door to be let in. We all know about middle children and middle cats. All of us except Louis—who opened the door and watched Ming rush into the house triumphantly with the biggest lizard you have ever seen in your life clutched in his jaws. Bright red blood spurted from every available artery the poor creature had.

Louis frantically dove for Ming. Ming, wondering why nobody was bragging on his prowess, let out a howl and released the severely injured lizard in the middle of our light gray carpet. Not knowing about 911, the lizard raced past the telephone and, you guessed it, under the icebox, leaving a bright red trail of blood all the way from the front door, through the living room and kitchen and under the frig. Everything got very, very quiet.

Ming sniffed around the icebox a couple of times, lost interest, and ambled into the dining room, where he jumped up on the sparkling waxed and buffed table, spread himself out as flat as he could get, and went to sleep on Louis' grandmother's hand tatted, white tablecloth.

The best laid plans of lizards and cats have oftimes gone astray.

Love,
Felix (or maybe Oscar)

July 11, 1998

Happy Birthday, My Friend—

No clever card—no jokes—no funny stories—just a <u>sincere</u> wish for you to be happy <u>every day</u> because you bring me much happiness just being who you are—a bright, sensitive, charming woman—decent, sweet, and yes, outrageous, too—creative, kind, compassionate—a soother to the pain of others, even when you are in pain yourself—a devoted mother, wife, sister—and a blessing, a <u>true</u> <u>reward</u>, to <u>all</u> of us lucky enough to know you.

My love to you,
Billie

When you reach the age of sixty, if you have one true friend . . .

July 13, 1998

Dear Billie,

In the fall of 1958, when I was a junior at the University of Oklahoma, Foster Harris, my creative writing professor, told our class, "When you reach the age of sixty, if you have one true friend . . . one person who, when called at midnight from the county jail to be told that you have committed murder, would not ask you, 'Did you do it?' but would say, 'I will come . . .' you will be quite fortunate indeed."

I, who was one and twenty, laughed at such absurdity and thought to myself, "I will have a host of friends . . . dozens of them . . . any one of which would come immediately and testify to my truthfulness . . . my honesty . . . my goodness . . . my purity of heart."

When I arrived at sixty, I discovered that Foster Harris was right . . . one it would be. And one would be enough. It was and is you, dear heart. And lest you feel that as a heavy burden, know that Sister will substitute for you at the jail whenever necessary. You just better pray that she outlives you.

I had a wonderful sixtieth, but my husband did not send me sixty red roses like Dennis did you when you passed that milestone in June. He didn't in spite of the fact that I told him your roses story many times. I can still smell your hotel room. Who would have thought that sixty roses would permeate the telephone wires?

Louis did give me a wonderful surprise. He bought me the seventeen oil paintings from Mike Wimmer's *Home Run, the Story of Babe Ruth*! You've met Mike at parties in the shop. He's the one who did the art for the *Lion King* video for Disney and the new Mr. Clean for Proctor and Gamble, among other things.

The main reason this is thrilling, besides the fact that I love the book, is that the gloves and cleats in the pictures

122

belong to me because they were my daddy's. Dad and Babe Ruth were the same age. I think I've told you that my dad was forty-five when I was born. Anyway, Mike always paints from life, and he borrowed Daddy's baseball gear, which I have saved all these years. So I was especially thrilled to own those oils with my dad's equipment pictured in them.

Since we issued your *The Honk and Holler, Opening Soon* with such a splash in June, my July 10th real anniversary went by quietly as I called your event my 11th Anniversary Celebration.

It was the best one I've ever had!

I'm sure glad to find out that you are older than I!

Molly

... one tiny patch beneath the west window.

August 5, 1998, the
62nd anniversary of my
brother Paul's birth

Dear Billie,

I left out one important story in my letter of June 20, 1996, when I told you about my last visit to the house where Sister and I grew up. We had sold the house, and I was doing one last walk-through looking for forgotten memories.

There was a full basement under the house, a basement where Sister and I spent many happy hours as little girls. That was the last place I went that hot July day. That basement was the coolest spot on earth in the summertime. When I say "on earth" I mean just that because the floor was dirt, black Oklahoma soil which, except for one tiny patch beneath the west window, had not felt the sun for over fifty years.

Daddy had built storage shelves down the middle and there were a few things left on them, things we had not had the room or the heart to carry upstairs the last time we were there together. This time I was alone, and the stuff needed to be gotten out.

Daddy's old shoe-shine box was there, still full of cans of Shinola and Griffin's polish along with the rag he used to buff our Mary Janes. On top of the shoe-shine box was a big brown sack from Levite's store filled with many smaller sacks carefully folded and stuck in there for future use.

On the shelf above was a little pile of match books which Sister had collected over the years on our trips to Texas to visit Mama's family. I scooped them into a big, chipped, enamel bowl, which was on the ground next to the shelves.

And finally, there was a once-white box, yellow with years, which contained our baby brother's pink satin blanket. On top of the bunny embroidered on the corner was the newspaper clipping of his obituary.

"Paul West Levite died Tuesday in Oklahoma City at the age of twenty days," it read. "He was the son of George and Lilly Levite." Less than two dozen words encompassed his entire life.

I packed up the shoe-shine box with my left hand, stuck the sack full of sacks under that arm, put Paul's blanket box under the other arm, grabbed the bowl of matches from the shelf, and trudged up the stairs.

When I got to the top of those worn basement stairs, I spied Daddy's old garden shovel propped in the corner of the back porch. I looked at it for a very long time.

Then I put down everything except Paul's blanket box and its precious contents, picked up Daddy's shovel and headed back downstairs. I walked to the west wall to the one little spot of sunshine which hit in the late afternoon and dug a hole. I placed the box which held our baby brother's little pink satin baby blanket with the bunny embroidered on it in the hole, covered it up with dirt, and began to cry.

That blanket had been in that box in that basement for forty-nine years. It just didn't seem right to take it out.

Molly

"... mayonnaise on his hot dog."

August 17, 1998

Dear Billie,

I'm so mad I could spit! A naked man ran into my friendly neighborhood Kinko's Copy shop last night, and I was not there. I spend half of my life in that Kinko's, but when something really good happens there, I'm at home. They did catch the guy on the store's video camera, but do you think they'd let me see it? *Noooo.* They claimed the police wouldn't even let the employees who weren't working when he came in see it, but I think they were just trying to keep him to themselves.

I even threatened to put a hurt on somebody unless they let me view it, but they still refused. Isn't that a great phrase—"put a hurt on"? I read it in a newspaper article about a couple of brothers who were in a fight with some other guys and Jim Bob says, "I had to hit him with the tire iron. They was really puttin' a hurt on my brother."

I missed that fight, too.

But back to Kinko's. Their naked man reminded me of Durant's naked man at the Dairy Queen, remember? You sent me the police report from the paper. You'll no doubt recall that the girl at the counter, when asked if there was anything unusual she could remember about her naked customer, replied, "Well, yes, he ordered mayonnaise on his hot dog." Contemplating her reply brings some most unusual images, doesn't it?

I'll close now and run back over to Kinko's. I plan to hang out there a lot more now just in case he comes back.

Love,
Molly

125

August 25, 1998

Dear Molly—

I'm returning all your letters as you requested, but it is breaking my heart. (Breaking up is so hard to do.)

I could not, however, make myself give up your senior ring which I will wear around my neck (though it is a <u>very</u> tight fit) until I take my last breath (which may be soon).

With all my love,
your steady—always,
Billie

. . . to get a phone call that makes you a mother is indescribable.

August 26, 1998

Dear Billie,

Twenty-eight years ago today, we brought Ginger Ann Griffis home from the adoption agency. It was the first ever "National Women's Liberation Day" and that made the news. Women from all over the nation were exhorted to take their children to the capitol buildings of their respective states and leave those children on the steps in protest over child care legislation which was pending.

"Listen to this," I read to Louis at breakfast that morning. "This article says that I am to take George (age three) to Oklahoma City and leave him on the steps of the capitol today."

"Ummm," says Louis, who is reading the sports page and munching toast.

"I think I'll do that," I say, wiping the food from the floor, the ceiling, the table, and everywhere else George has managed to fling it. He was really a messy kid. "Maybe one of those legislators will clean up after him for a day or two."

"Ummm," says Louis.

"As much as I love George, I think it's the least I can do to support my Liberated Sisters."

"Ummmm," says Louis.

He leaves for work, and at 11:05 the phone rings. It is Jane Conner from the adoption agency.

"Hi, this is Jane Conner, and I'm holding your daughter in my lap," she says. "How soon can you come and get her?"

Unless you have been there, there are no words in the language—and I know a lot of words—which can express a mama's feelings at that time. Elation? Much too calm. Joy? Far too short. Totally wild and amazing, astounding and astonishing—those don't even touch it. Even if those words have been said before (it was Jane who had called us about George) to get a phone call that makes you a mother is indescribable. So I won't even try.

By 1:00 we were there, and Jane was putting our daughter in my arms, Louis was saying, "I'm your Daddy," and George was carefully examining the clothes and toys which came with her.

"She's a redhead!" I exclaimed. "My Uncle Bill is a redhead."

"Oh, it won't stay that color," Jane said. "That's baby hair."

But stay it did. And because of it, we named her Ginger.

On that wonderful, hot summer day we drove home in our last un-airconditioned car. It was 110 in the shade and hotter than that in our car. Ginger cried most of the way home.

"The next car we get will have air conditioning," I remember Louis saying. No daughter of his was going to have to sweat.

When we got home, Louis reminded me that I was going to take George and place him on the capitol steps.

"Are you sure you can get two of them up there?" he teased.

"We went right past the capitol when we left the agency," I pointed out. "I don't think I really wanted to be liberated."

What a day. Oh, what a day!

Molly the Mama

It was not the food I missed. It was the stories.

September 10, 1998

Dear Sister Billie,

I have always wondered why the arrival of suppertime very often washes an enormous wave of homesickness over my soul. Supper is the evening meal for those of us from small towns. In big towns like Tulsa where you grew up I'll bet it was called dinner. This yearning happens even when I am in my own home surrounded by my own family. Warm, well-fed, and almost content.

Tonight I think I figured it out. I was sitting on the patio thinking about the hundreds and hundreds of suppers my sweet Mama must have cooked for us during my growing up years. Supper was the only meal of the day where all four of us were together. Daddy went to work quite early and cooked his own breakfast. Mama slept late and didn't eat breakfast, so Sister cooked my breakfast. It usually consisted of burned toast which she scraped when I demanded that she do so, or oatmeal which was always undercooked. I couldn't find a cure for that.

Anyway, here I am, a grown-up sixty-year-old woman, totally gray haired and homesick as a little kid at summer camp. Then it hit me.

It was not the food I missed. It was the stories.

We told them in age order. Daddy went first. He told about the store—the customers, the funny things they said and did, the irritating things they said and did. His newspaper articles. His day. And we loved it. Then Mama revealed all the drug store gossip which was fit for young ears. She edited it because of Sister and me, and waited to tell Daddy the "rest of the story" when they were snuggled in bed that night.

Then Sister told what happened at school—who threw up in the line waiting for a drink of water, what Miss Smith yelled at Billy Clyde on the playground, all that stuff.

Then it was MY turn. I, the original coffee table dancer, amazed and mesmerized them all with tales of having to beat the chalk erasers because I talked too much ... of having to sit under the sand table for half of the arithmetic lesson for having talked too much ... of having to ... well, you get the picture. And they listened and smiled. And they loved me. For having talked too much.

And then I knew why Louis couldn't understand my homesickness. And why it was the food which was important to him. Even now, his sweet Mama sends us food each and every night, food of some kind or another. But not any stories. Somehow I don't think they told stories at their table. Louis is, by nature, a very quiet and private person.

Cooking up a good story was a finely honed art in my first family. It's not the food that I miss. It's my audience.

Molly G.

. . . real people answering real phones.

September 30, 1998

Dear Billie again!

I hate having to address letters to you in California! It makes you seem so very far away, which of course you are!

How is the screen script coming? I still think it is amazing that they hired you and Tracy to write the script for your very own book. Does that happen very often? I've never heard of it.

I am sitting here with sweat running down my face because I was dancing to "You Ain't Woman Enough to Take My Man," my favorite song next to "Don't Call Him a Cowboy Until You See Him Ride" or maybe Lawrence Welk's "Pennsylvania Polka," which I save for special occasions like the Jewish New Year of 5759 which I am celebrating as we speak, read, or type!

Anyway, I had to write and tell you what a wonderful bunch those guys at Time Warner Books are. But you no doubt know that by now. Unlike some of the companies I deal with, they have real people answering real phones and seem willing to bend over backward to help me. As I often tell you, little independent bookshops such as mine have to depend on "the kindness of strangers" as the waif in *Les Misérables* said.

Anyway, they co-op ads for me, let me order in odd and wild numbers, send me promo material—the whole full meal deal. And I just wanted to tell you that so you could pass it on. It is greatly appreciated by "The Shop Around the Corner." Have you ever seen that old movie? I identify with that story.

M. G.

". . . the author who wrote one, and then another one."

October 10, 1998

Dear Billie,

Yesterday, a ditsy woman who was in school with me at OU charged in the door of the shop and said, "I need another one of those books from you. The one by the author who wrote one, and then wrote another one."

"Billie Letts?" queries I, not even stopping to think awhile.
"That's the one!" says she.

Now I ask you, would that ever happen in Borders or Barnes and Noble?

It would not. And it certainly would not happen in Wal-Mart!

This same woman had a daughter in my son's class during the grade-school years. They were in the fifth grade when this incident, related to me by both the teacher and my son, occurred. Ditz's daughter (What a great book title: *Ditz's Daughter*) had a kidney infection which necessitated frequent trips to the bathroom. The mother had cautioned the teacher about this fact and instructed the teacher to allow the girl to go "anytime she takes a notion."

A few days later the mother appeared at the door of the classroom waving a small, empty specimen bottle in the air and gesticulating come-here signals to her mortified daughter. Her fellow fifth graders were delighted.

The poor girl excused herself, followed her mother down the hall to the girls' restroom, filled the bottle, and returned to face the derision of her classmates who had not an ounce of sympathy for her. Fifth graders are heartless.

So now you know why, when the lady said she wanted "another book by that woman who wrote one and then wrote another one," I knew exactly what books she meant.

Perhaps it takes one to know one.

Love,
Molly

December 1, 1998

Dear Billie:

Topic: Shifting of roles
Subject: Louis Griffis
      (maybe this should be Molly, I'm not sure)

    I have discovered that my millions in royalties will not come from "The Letts Letters," but from a *How to Survive Retirement of Your Husband* and *Run Away with the Milkman* subtitled: *There Are No Competent Milkmen*, which is a really depressing thought.

    The mail on Thursday contained a packet from the U.S.A.A. Insurance Company (Louis is retired military, remember?). That is one of the many reasons that I am a registered Republican and salute the flag every time I see it when I am driving down the street. That and the fact that Daddy was in the American Legion, and I was the governor of Girls' State.) In this packet from the insurance company were the little forms one is to put in the glove compartment of the car, and the duplicate which goes in the file cabinet.

    For the thirty-eight years of my marriage, I have put these little Jessies in the glove box (his term) or glove compartment (my term) and the file cabinet. I, as I always do, capriciously put the very important one labeled "PRESENT THIS TO YOUR TAG AGENT WHEN PURCHASING YOUR TAG" or some such admonition, either under "A" for automobile, "C" for car, or "I" for important, which is where I file most things, not being able, at the time of receipt, to determine which of the letters of the alphabet is the appropriate recipient of the thing I am required by law (Louis Law) to file. If it were not for him, I would toss it all away and now be serving time in the penitentiary at McAlester.

    So, in retirement plus two months, I open this packet and say to him, "Since you have so much more time on your hands than I, I think you can take care of the car insurance verification stuff."

"I thought that was your job," he replies, turning the page of his *Wall Street Journal*, to which, until last month Kerr-McGee subscripted for him. Now he forks out seventy-five cents a day for that paper which, as I see it, we can ill afford. He sips his coffee and reads it while I pile my arthritic-ridden body into my car and head for another day of harassment from people who do not understand why I do not stock copies of *The Life and Times of Hattie Smarty, the Smartest Woman in Coal County*, compiled by her adoring grandchildren.

"Your newspaper ads claim that you specialize in THE UNIQUE!" says Hattie the II, named for her grandmother. "I can't believe you don't have it! You had a really big deal for somebody named Letts last summer, and I've never even heard of her."

I stave myself from pointing out that her grandmother self-published (I am guessing, but I'm sure I am right) and that her grandmother gave away 1,583 copies of her memoir to the relatives she liked (or could tolerate) at her "Release of Potential Best Seller" party at the local Wal-Mart in a town which shall remain unnamed.

That same store, by the by, refused to host my friend Billie Letts, author of *Where the Heart Is* and *The Honk and Holler, Opening Soon*.

"Mrs. Letts' book," says I, "had a full-page COLOR ad in PEOPLE MAGAZINE."

"Gran asked me to pay for one of those," says Hattie II, "but since she didn't invite me to her premier signing, I refused."

Louis reads the *Wall Street Journal* while I put up with the likes of Hattie II.

I left those automobile forms on the dining room table for eight days, and finally, resigned to my fate, cut at the appropriate line, marched to the four cars involved, and deposited the correct little rectangle into each GLOVE COMPARTMENT.

I marched into the kitchen where HE was still engrossed in the *Wall Street Journal* and asked, "Do you want these car things filed under "A" for automobile, or "C" for car, or "I" for insurance?"

133

He did not miss a beat or feel the least chagrined as he replied, "'I' for insurance."

And I promise you that, one year from now, when he has to find the things for one reason or another, he will say, "Where in the world did you put those insurance papers?"

Wanna bet?

Me!

Oprah's Choice

December 7, 1998

Hello, Buckeyed Billie!

I started to leave the entire first page of this letter blank just so you would know that your phone call left me momentarily speechless! But speechless is not wordless, and I have never been wordless. Even my favorite line, "I'm so excited my nipples itch," doesn't do justice to your amazing news.

Oprah's Choice.

That makes me itch all over! How many times did you say "Oprah's Choice" in the first hours and days after she called? It's like being crowned "Queen for a Day" without having to lug a washing machine home. (I always thought they should have given her a maid for life.)

My dear friend, it couldn't have happened to a nicer lady. You've been my and Sister's and lots and lots of other people's "choice" for a long time, but this event will spread your fame not only as a fine writer, but also as a good, good person because people see the goodness in you when they read your words. Think how proud Novalee, Sister Husband, and Forney are.

Your rendition of Oprah's call and your response was made for prime time TV. Were you pinching yourself the whole time she was talking to you? When you called, I was so excited I forgot to ask if Dennis were there when she called. Was he? If not, how long did it take you to locate him? What were his first words? The best part of Dennis is that he'd rather have something wonderful happen to you than to himself.

Well, I know you have better things to do right now than sit around reading letters, so I'll close for the moment. But do know that just like Dennis, I would rather it have happened to you than to me.

Almost.

My wonderful old Aunt Opal taught me many things. One of those things was not to ever say that I was lucky.

"Oh, no, my dear," she would say, "don't ever say that you are lucky. Say you are blessed." She always corrected me when I'd tell her how lucky I was to have Louis, how lucky we were to get George, how lucky we were to get Ginger.

So I'll correct my salutation and say you are not "Buckeyed" because that would mean you were lucky. You are blessed. (Emphasis the first syllable. BLESSed, not blessED.) The blessED shall inherit the earth, and a lot of other stuff like that, and you sure as heck don't want the earth to take care of. Dennis is going to be enough to keep you busy.

> Love you,
> Molly

December 12, 1998

My dream last night:

I was on my way to some event at which I was the featured speaker. A big event! But as I arrived, I discovered that I hadn't shaved my legs—for weeks—for months—for years. My legs were covered with hair ... long, tangled, matted! No place to shave, no time to shave and nothing to shave with. Nothing to do but climb onto the stage and deliver my speech—with hairy legs—hoping no one would notice.

Were you there, Molly? Were you in that audience? Did you look at my legs?

> Love to you,
> Billie

December 15, 1998

Billie Letts
c/o Los Angeles County Correctional Institute
100093 West 1052 St.
Los Angeles, CA 80932

Dear Ms. Letts,

Your friend and confidant, the infamous children's writer Molly Levite Griffis, has forwarded your recent dream letter to me in the hope that I can, in some way, help you before you shame not only your husband and sons, but also your two adopted sisters by appearing on the Oprah Winfrey show with the hair on your legs in braids.

By the oddest of coincidences, the night of your hairy leg dream I had the VERY SAME DREAM. I was in the front row of the auditorium when you drug your matted legs (along with the rest of your body, fortunately) up to the podium and began to speak. I, who like to think that I have been and dreamed everything there is to be or dream, said to myself, "Is she innately ill-bred, or is she just trying to shame the Gillette razor company?"

While highly creative people often have dreams which are difficult for me to interpret, yours I must say is of the common garden variety dream. Legs, hair, auditorium—I've heard it all before.

I would therefore suggest that you stop drinking milk after 1:00 on weekdays, avoid chocolate, and green beans all together, and join a Weight Watchers group immediately. I feel certain that they have someone there who shaves the legs of each and every client just before he or she weighs in.

While not shaving one's legs is not, in and of itself, reason for incarceration, lack of attention to detail in one part of one's life often leads to similar inattention in other areas. SOME people begin to fail to sign their checks after they have made them out. You fall into this category. Because infamous children's author MOLLY LEVITE GRIFFIS has grown rather fond of you over the years, she regretted having to turn your unsigned check over to the Los Angeles Police Department, but as the old saying goes, "Business is business!" Once again you have displayed your total lack of creativity. Not signing one's checks in order to postpone the payment of one's debts is the oldest ploy in the world, Ms. Letts. And insanity, temporary or permanent, is no excuse. Ms. Griffis and I both fervently hope that you will be released in time to make your appearance on the Oprah Winfrey show, but should you not make it, Ms. Griffis has graciously consented to appear in your place. Her legs will be shaved.

Dr. Strange Love

[This was mailed with an envelope filled with autographed book plates.]

December 22, 1998

Just stick one of these on my unsigned check!
Have a wonderful Christmas!

I Love You,

_____
SIGNATURE

W.W.M.D.—
What Would Martha Do?

January 5, 1999

Dear Billie,

Since I know how wild your impending Oprah visit has made your life, I decided to write you again instead of calling you every five minutes and tying up your telephone line. Had you thought of adding "call interrupt," or has your life been interrupted enough already? I think that is the case.

I feel guilty that I have called you so many times since December 7, but it is all so exciting I can't stand to not know how you are reacting. What I would have called to tell you today was the first line of your next novel, which is to be: "Mary Ellen knew that the New Year was not going to be all she wished it to be when she burned the black-eyed peas she was fixing for dinner." Good, huh? Do all your friends tell you what to write as much as I do?

Actually, the black-eyed pea burning did happen to poor Sister. She was packing away the Christmas stuff while holding and reading Martha Stewart's article about the importance of packing Christmas trappings away in the proper manner. Now that she knew it was required, Sister was carefully marking each ornament, each recipe, each piece of wrapping paper with labels; i.e., "This egg carton section, liberally slathered with gold glitter, was made by Cheri at the Centenary Methodist Church Sunday school in 1959 (Cheri was three) under the auspices of Mrs. Robert B. Storms, teacher of the Cherub Class. There are no decorations made by Cindy as she was the third child and no one saves anything done by third children."

Until this year, Sister had not known that such markings were necessary. But if Martha Stewart said you should pack carefully and wisely, Sister would pack carefully and wisely.

Sister worships at Martha's feet. In her off moments, she has dreamed of designing a bracelet with the letters, W.W.M.D., standing for What Would Martha Do, but was sure that some of her more devout friends might take offense and think she was making fun of the What Would Jesus Do movement. Which, of course, she would be. Kind of. But not really. It takes all kinds, Sister says. Lots of folks put Martha Stewart right up on the right hand of God, and that's OK with Sister. Even if it was Martha's fault that she burned the black-eyed peas.

As they says in the sports world, "Wait 'til next year!"

Love,
Molly

". . . from the bottom of my heart."

Billie kept saying she was going to thank Molly for helping her, so Molly mailed a note card to Billie which stated "Thank you from the bottom of my heart" on the outside. On the inside, she wrote:

January 5, 1999

My dearest Molly-O,

Thank you from the bottom of my heart (and other bottoms) for your <u>enthusiastic</u> selling of my books, <u>Where the Heart Is</u> and <u>The Honk & Holler, Opening Soon</u>. Of the thousands of book sellers I know, I love you best!

Sign here! → _____

BILLIE LETTS

Billie's reply:

Number 1!

January 7, 1999

Dear Billie,

Well, you did it today!

Number 1 on Best Seller lists across the U.S.A.!

Good grief, as Charlie Brown says, and to think I know you—have slept in your house. Would you mind putting up a little plaque on your front door to that effect: "Molly Griffis Slept Here" will do. I'd appreciate it.

When I read your name on that list I remembered the story you told me on the phone last week when W.T.H.I. had risen to number 5 on *U.S.A. Today*. I like to call it that because that's how they shorten GONE WITH THE WIND—initials only. And when your movie is made, that's what they'll do! Anyway, I remembered you telling me how, when it first came out, you paid *U.S.A. Today* $80 to get their top 150 faxed to

140

you each Thursday. I sat and looked at your number-one title and pictured you, way back in 1995, sitting in your car in front of the fax place and starting at number 150 and making your way up the list with your heart in your throat. And you weren't there! And now you are!

You've come a long way, Baby.

Love,
Molly

January 10, 1999

Headin' Home!
Got Okla in my blood!
Riding the plains once more!
In them Oklahoma hills
    where I was born!
Home, Home on the Range!
You're the reason God made
    Oklahoma!
Where the wavin' wheat, it
    sure smells sweet!
Home is the place where
    your history begins!

—Billie

January 12, 1999

Dear Billie,

I figured by this time you were getting so much mail that I had better fax any Letts Letters or you wouldn't be reading my pearls of wisdom until your eyesight had already failed you!

And just in case you are getting so many faxes you don't have time to read them all, I used stationery which was sure to grab your attention! My sheet has *The Honk and Holler* in red, by the way. Too bad you don't have a color printer on your fax or you would really be impressed.

Well, "the best laid plans of mice and men," as the old saying goes (I'm sure you, like me, figured out long ago that the plans in that old saying went astray because they had MEN doing the planning). And it was some MAN at *The Daily Oklahoman* who printed a story about you done by a stringer instead of by Anne DeFrange, to whom I had given all the correct details! So, the story which ran with a wonderful color picture of the cover of *Where the Heart Is* and the glamorous shot of you (personally, I like the one taken by Dennis in the barn better) on the front page of the "Entertainment" section says that you will be on Oprah this Friday, January 15 instead of the new date of Tuesday, January 19. But I called and straightened them out! I also called Anne Morris at *The Austin American-Statesman* as she has given you such nice coverage.

But the most important call I made was to the Warner Brothers, each and every one of them, to tell them that those guys taking the orders for *Where the Heart Is* were not telling the bookstores that the book was also available in hardback again! And just in case The Brothers don't have a real handle on things, I also called Tina A. and various folks at Warner Books who actually take the orders to explain that ten percent of $17.95 was much preferable to ten percent of $12. by anybody's mathematical calculations, even poor Sister's!

To cover all bases, I got that neat Luis Rivera at Warner's to agree to co-op some ads in the newspapers telling the correct day and time!

Am I good, or what?

Love,
Molly

P.S. I know you keep telling me that Warner Books is not the same bunch as Warner Brothers, but what do you know? We need to cover all the bases!

Today is my 75th wedding anniversary . . .

January 22, 1999

Dear Billie,

Today is my 75th wedding anniversary and nobody has even noticed. You'd think, with the 75th being the Diamond one, that our kids would have flown in from all over the world to throw us a surprise party or something. Even Louis, who is usually pretty good about presents, said that now that he was retired, he was too broke to buy me anything. I think he's taking his retirement too seriously.

You do remember the story we told you over dinner one night last year about our first wedding, don't you? But then again, when you have friends who are celebrating their 75th anniversary, your memory may not be what it used to be, so I'll refresh it.

Sister got married in a big church wedding with six or seven bridesmaids, two wedding cakes, tuxedos, and our mother, who loved every minute of planning it. Daddy, who was a very plain man, was miserable. After all the hoopla was over, Daddy took me aside and told me that when I decided to get married, he would give me $500 if I'd elope. Back then $500 was a bunch of money, as you know. Sounded like a great plan to me.

So, some six years later when Louis and I decided to tie the knot, I told him about Daddy's proposal. Louis was elated. He, like Daddy, is a plain person. When we finished our last finals of the last semester of my senior year at OU, we eloped to Henrietta, Texas. The next weekend, I went home alone to tell Daddy and get him to help me tell Mama, who would not be at all pleased, I was sure.

I made a big mistake in the way I started the conversation. Instead of blurting out, "Daddy, we eloped!" I said, "Daddy, do you remember how you told me that if I would elope instead of having a big wedding, you'd give me $500?"

To which he replied, "Oh, Molly, I know I told you that, but I mentioned that once to your mother, and she had one of her hissy fits and said you couldn't do that. She wants another fancy wedding, so we'd better go along with her."

And so we did. Three months later, in the First Christian Church of Apache, Molly Sue Levite and Louis Reginald Griffis got married. Again. With a bunch of bridesmaids, and two cakes and a very happy mother who planned it all.

And who died never knowing about my elopement. I just never found a time when I thought she'd think it was funny.

Since that first elopement took place in January of 1960 and the second wedding in April of that same year, we have celebrated two wedding anniversaries each year. That makes today our first 38th anniversary or the 75th time we have toasted each other, see? Diamonds are forever, right?

Molly

I suggest approaching Morton's Salt Company to underwrite you.

January 30, 1999

Dear Billie,

It was good to get your call last night and to find that you are starting novel #3 on Monday! I passed that information on to Sister, who thought your timing was absolutely perfect. Sunday night there is not only a full moon, but a full Blue Moon for her to dance nude under. I warned her that HER moon was going to be blue if she kept that up, but she says no sacrifice is too great to ward off writer's block for you.

Now while I draw the line several feet before nude dancing, I will give you the benefit of my creative juices by sending along the following synopsis just in case you are still sitting in front of your typewriter waiting for the muse to whisper in your ear.

SALT OF THE EARTH
(possible title)

There's this very nice, very sweet, very kind, hard-working woman named Mortonia who drags her aching body out of bed each morning and trudges off to work in a salt mine deep in the bowels of the earth. She works seven days a week (and more in some months) from early in the morning until late at night.

She has this husband who is retired. All day long he does nothing. Absolutely nothing AT ALL except eat, drink, and be merry.

One dark and stormy night poor Mortonia is trudging through the rain in her yellow slicker, huddled under her giant umbrella trying to fend off the driving rain and muttering to herself, "When it rains, it pours." She sighs a deep sigh and thinks to herself, sweetly and kindly, "If

145

that Son of a Bitch is sitting there sipping a Martini when I walk in, he's dead meat."

I think you can let your own imagination take over from there. Start thinking in salty terms: "pour salt in the wound" (murder mystery) ... "take it with a grain of salt" (cookbook or philosophy) ... "the salt of the earth" or "if the salt hath lost its savor" (religious) ... "please pass the salt" (etiquette) ... "I wanna be your salty dog" (musical) ... The possibilities are endless.

As you might have noticed, I always write with marketing ideas in mind, so if you use my plot idea (which I give to you free and clear), I suggest approaching the Morton's Salt Company to underwrite you. The subliminal advertising going on here ought to really appeal to them.

Your spicy friend,
Molly